MY VIOLIN NEEDS HELP!

A repair diagnostics guide for players and teachers

Copyright © 2020 Korinthia A. Klein
All rights reserved.
Cover art by Barrett Klein
Photographs by Korinthia A. Klein

Except as permitted under the US Copyright Act of 1976, no part of this book may be reproduced, distributed or transmitted in any form or by any means, or stored in a database or retrieval system, without the prior written permission of the publisher.

ISBN-13: 978-1-7333889-5-5
Manufactured in the United States of America

This book is dedicated to all the players curious about their instruments, and the teachers who continue to learn themselves.

MY VIOLIN NEEDS HELP!

A repair diagnostics guide for players and teachers

by Korinthia A. Klein

TABLE OF CONTENTS

Introduction	1
Chapter 1: Vocabulary	5
Chapter 2: Strings 'N Things	39
Chapter 3: Glue	63
Chapter 4: Varnish	65
Chapter 5: Tracking Down a Buzz	69
Chapter 6: What to Know about Your Bow	79
Chapter 7: Notes about Cellos	89
Chapter 8: Quick Tips for Teachers in Schools	95
Chapter 9: Additional Dos and Don'ts	113
Chapter 10: Recap of Basic Maintenance	119
Acknowledgments	123
References	124
Index	126

INTRODUCTION

My name is Korinthia Klein, and I am a luthier. A luthier is a person who builds and/or repairs stringed instruments. The term originates from people who worked on lutes, but today generally refers to violin and guitar makers. I, myself, am a violist and proud of it, but for simplicity's sake, I'm going to use the word "violin" in this book to mean violin, viola, or cello. (Basses are a whole different story that I am not prepared to address in any depth. Someone else will have to write that book.)

I come at violin from a lot of angles. I learned violin in public school, switched to viola in high school, and majored in music in college where I got a BA degree with distinction in Music Cognition. I then went on to violin making school, where I supported myself by teaching private and group lessons. I am the parent of kids who play, I have observed and assisted other teachers in action, I played in a professional string quartet for a long time, and currently perform with a civic orchestra. I build, repair, sell, rent, and I have done a lot of volunteer work on instruments for our public school system, in addition to paid contract work. I've seen a lot of violins, some spectacular, and some that barely qualify as real instruments. They all need work at some point or another.

I know what it's like to play, perform, and teach, and still not understand how our instruments work. Having gone to violin making school then worked in repair shops for decades, I now realize how little I knew. I want to share information that I wish I'd had back when I was a player and teacher and trying to advise students, before I became a luthier.

There are simple things people can adjust by themselves at home that make using and caring for your instrument much easier. However, I also see a lot of problems caused by well-intentioned people trying to fix things on their own, usually in an attempt to save themselves time and money, but it winds up costing them more of both. I want people to understand their instruments well enough to know when they can do something themselves, and when not to. I want to share information that I believe will help.

So as we begin, let me tell you what this book will and won't do:

This book will not qualify you to do repair work on violins. There are no shortcuts to being a luthier, just as there are no shortcuts to being a player. This book will also not go into great detail about how violins are made, their history, or delve much beyond the surface of certain repairs. There are better resources for that, and I hope you investigate them, because all of it is fascinating.

It will, I hope, help you understand these wonderful instruments of the violin family better, and empower you to diagnose problems properly, as well as perform simple maintenance tasks that should preserve the health of your violin, viola, or cello. If someone avoids a possible repair disaster, or even just feels better informed as they take their instrument in for work, this book will have been worth my effort.

Also, it helps going into this to have some perspective on what level of precision is required for your instrument before you decide who should attempt adjustments. It matters if a violin belongs to you, or someone else. If your instrument is valuable, either because of its price tag or sentimental component, I wouldn't advise you risk doing much yourself. If you are dealing with cheap student instruments, you have more latitude.

No one can claim to know it all, and I am humbled every day by how much more I still have to learn. Luthiers often have differing opinions about their craft, so I don't expect them all to agree on everything here. However, we all have to start somewhere, and I am offering up basic knowledge formed from my education and continuing experience. I hope it proves useful.

The aim of this book is to be a practical resource, and a place to turn when a violin has a problem in order to figure out what to do next. If you want to save some time and get the gist of this book now, simply remember that when in doubt? Take it to a luthier.

That said, let's examine the most common things I wish all players knew so we can work together to keep our instruments running well, and keep making music.

CHAPTER 1

VOCABULARY

If you're involved enough with violin playing that you picked up this book, many of these terms should already be familiar. Others may not. But I am a firm believer in having an accurate vocabulary in order to avoid misunderstandings and to get the answers you need. It helps when players, students, and teachers use the same terms as luthiers in order to communicate. It also helps to know how to describe different types of damage or repairs with words everyone agrees on. We're all better off if we can talk to each other knowledgeably and on the same page.

Please keep in mind that I live and work in the Midwestern region of the United States. I am aware of other terms used in other English speaking parts of the world, as well as regional differences in my own country. So if, for instance, you learned the word "belly" instead of "top" when talking about the piece of spruce that the front of your instrument is made of, that's perfectly fine. I'm going to focus on the terms that are common here among the people I work with in my industry, but if any of these don't match your experience, ask your local luthier what terms they use so you are able to communicate better where you live.

Let's begin with the handout that I provide to beginners when they rent a violin or viola from our store. These are the terms, in my experience, most likely to be needed by a new player when taking lessons. It's a more complete list than I usually see offered in basic books or handouts in schools, but there are certainly many more terms to know, and I will add some of those as we work our way down the instrument. I also want to introduce into this vocabulary list the names of basic repairs and procedures that every player should be familiar with.

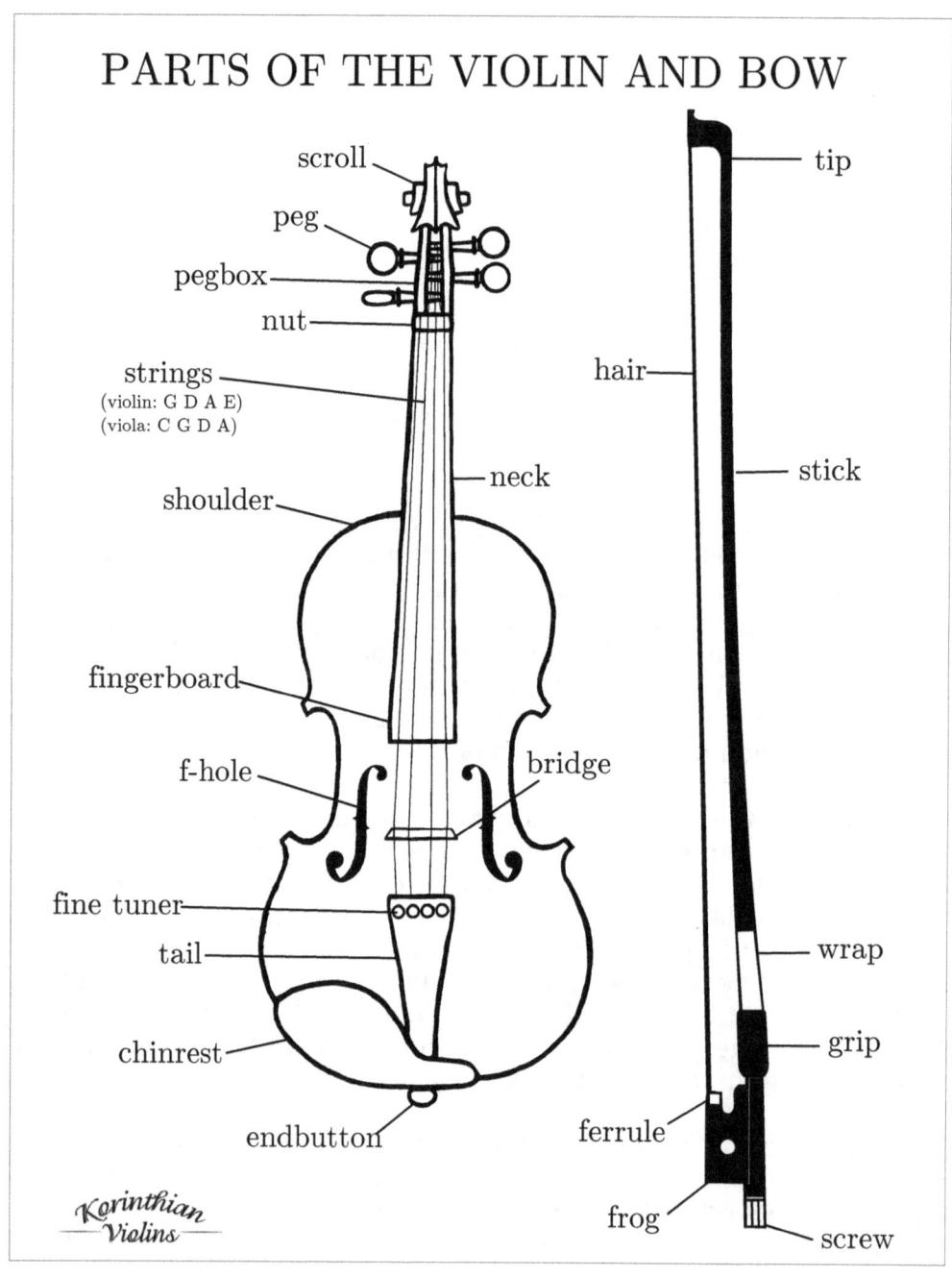

SCROLL

Let's start up top with that scroll. Technically, only that part at the end curling into a spiral is the scroll, but if you call that whole area including the pegs "the scroll" no one will mind. The scroll has a first turn, a second turn and an eye. The scooped areas that run around the front of the scroll and down the back behind the pegbox is called the volute. The scroll is usually made of maple. If you have a really cheap violin, the second turn and eye may be plastic.

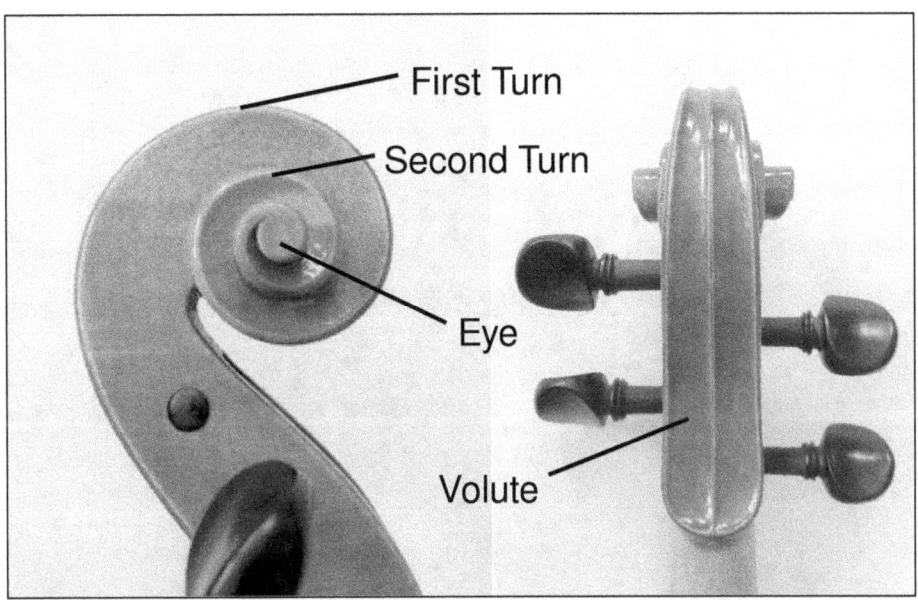

It's a point of pride among makers to carve a really beautiful scroll, because symmetry is hard. But in terms of function, the scroll should have a certain amount of mass that helps the instrument resonate properly, so if your scroll breaks off, that's bad. Do not glue it back on yourself, or let someone who does other kinds of woodworking do it. Take it to a luthier. Because it's also likely that any kind of trauma that had enough force to break off a scroll, impacted other things on the instrument the average player doesn't know how to check.

(If you're interested, I think Nicolo Amati made the world's most beautiful scrolls. This scroll pictured to the right is a favorite that I photographed on a visit to the National Music Museum in Vermillion SD. The violin was made in 1628.)

PEGBOX

The pegbox is the area that holds the pegs. No musician I know has ever taken notice of the inside of their pegbox. For me, it's the most annoying part of a violin to carve. It's tricky, it's awkward, and it's under-appreciated. What should you know about the inside of the pegbox? That not enough clearance at the bottom of it is the most common cause of strings not staying in the pegs.

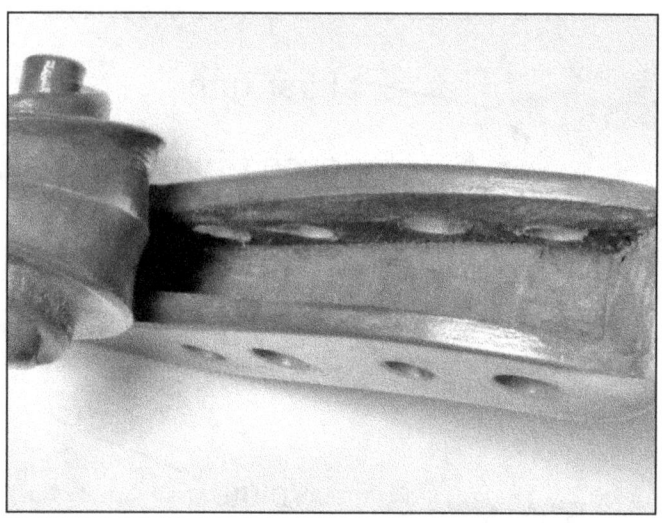

PEGS

Parts of the peg itself include the shaft, the head, the string hole (not pictured because this is an unfitted peg), the collar, and sometimes the decorative ball at the end, which is often called a "pip." (But saying "the little ball on the end" works.)

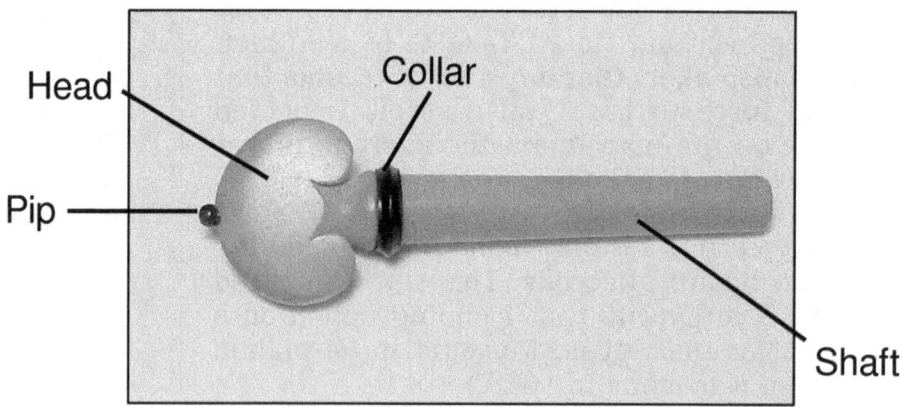

If your peg also includes a large screw on the end, you have my sympathy. They are likely Caspari pegs, a defunct brand of mechanical peg which one fellow repair person I know refers to as "The Devil's Peg." They are awful, and when they fail they are miserable to deal with. They are the wild card in any repair estimate, because you can never be sure when they are going to go, so it can be hard to know if putting money into other repairs on the same instrument is worth the gamble.

FILE FITTING A NEW PEG

Pegs have to be specially fitted to the particular hole they are in. We do that with several different tools, including a hand file. You can't just buy a new peg if one of yours breaks and expect it to work in the old hole. If you have a broken peg, take it to a luthier.

As pegs work their way across the pegbox with use, they need to be replaced with new pegs with larger shafts to fit the now slightly larger holes. I would say on average that a typical violin goes through about three sets of pegs before the holes are too large to file fit new replacements. (At that point you need a pegbox bushing.)

File fitting new pegs is also the procedure that happens when you simply want to replace pegs for aesthetic reasons.

PEGBOX BUSHING

If you need new pegs, but the holes in the pegbox have over time become too large to accommodate pegs of reasonable size, you need a pegbox bushing. This is an involved repair where the pegbox holes are filled with boxwood, re-varnished, and new smaller holes are reamed to fit new smaller pegs. It's common on old instruments, rare on newer ones.

NUT and FINGERBOARD

Moving on down, the nut and fingerboard should both be made of ebony—a black wood which is dense enough to withstand a lot of wear. It's common on cheap violins that one or both of these are made of softer wood that is painted black, which doesn't work as well. On some older instruments, they can also be made from rosewood, which is pretty, but harder to work with.

The fingerboard is the surface you press the strings against when you use your fingers to create different pitches. The nut's job is to hold the strings up off that end of the fingerboard. The strings should not sit too deeply into the nut, or be breaking over the curve of it sharply.

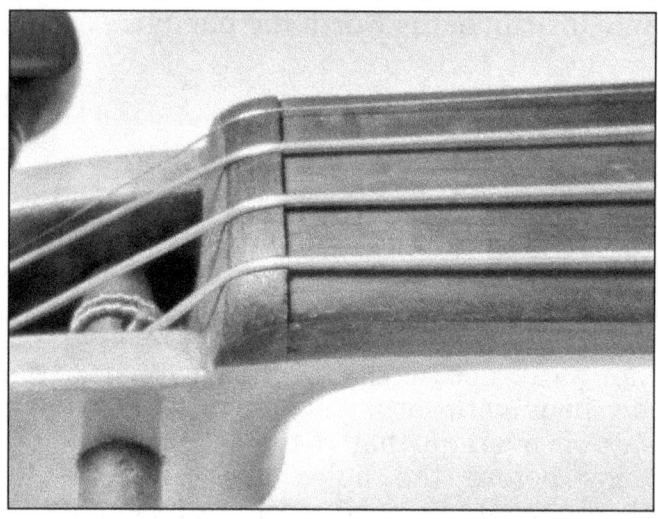

FINGERBOARD DRESSING

This is one of the most common jobs I do in my shop, and the least likely to be something players have heard of. Over time, you can wear pits and grooves into the fingerboard with the repeated pressure of your fingers and strings. Dressing a fingerboard means replaning its surface and polishing it out again.

Fingerboards are shaped to a specific curve across their width and scooped in their length. Luthiers check these with templates and a straightedge. Most players aren't aware that any maintenance needs to happen with their fingerboards, but it's an important part of any basic checkup.

How often this needs to be done depends on several factors, including the composition of your sweat, the porosity of the particular piece of wood, and how much you play. I have some clients who need their board dressed about every other year, some every ten years, some never. It's a thing a luthier should check for you and is good for players to know about.

NECK

Behind the fingerboard is the neck.

I think the most surprising thing for the average player to learn about their violin, is that the neck is not considered a permanent part of the instrument. Few really old instruments have their original neck. Replacing a neck requires a "neck graft" where you cut off the scroll and saw out the neck at the button. The button is part of the back plate—that little bump that attaches to the neck heel. The scroll is then mounted onto a new piece of wood that you shape and fit back onto the body.

From a general repair standpoint, it's good to know that necks can be reshaped. If the neck on your instrument is uncomfortable in some way, or too thick, it's not a big deal to reshape it. This is not considered an alteration that impacts the integrity of the instrument as a whole.

The neck is not varnished the same way as the rest of the violin, since the constant contact with your hand and sweat would wear through that. There are several accepted options for finishing a neck. I usually tint the wood with some color, then polish it out with shellac which is durable and easily re-applied.

If the neck is coming out of your instrument, loosen all the strings to relieve tension. If the neck is simply unglued, that should be a simple fix and something your luthier can turn around pretty fast. If the button has broken away from the back plate and is coming off with the neck, that is a serious injury, and not so simple to repair.

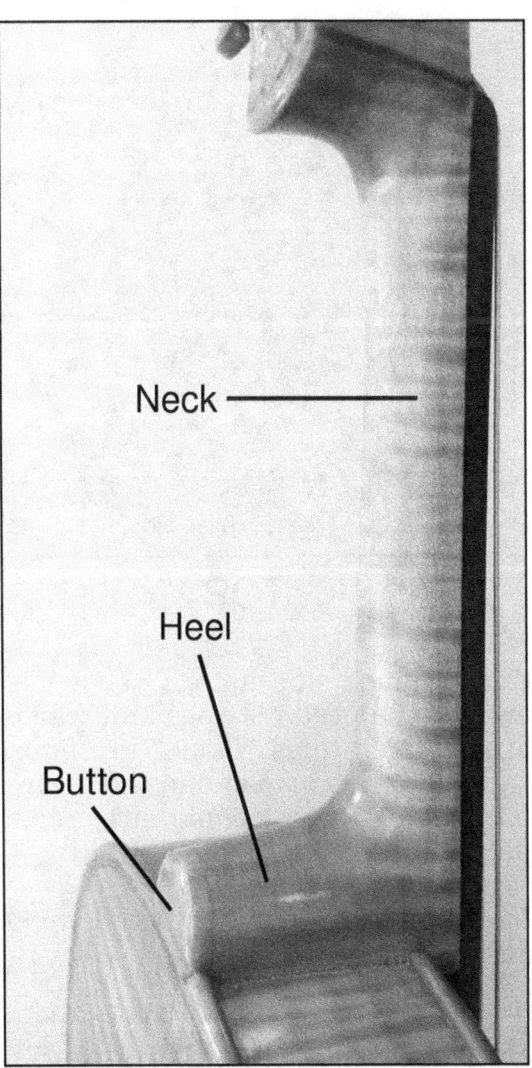

TOP and BACK

Moving on down to the basic body of the instrument: The body has two "plates." The front plate is made of spruce and is referred to as the "top." The reverse side, usually made of maple, is the "back."

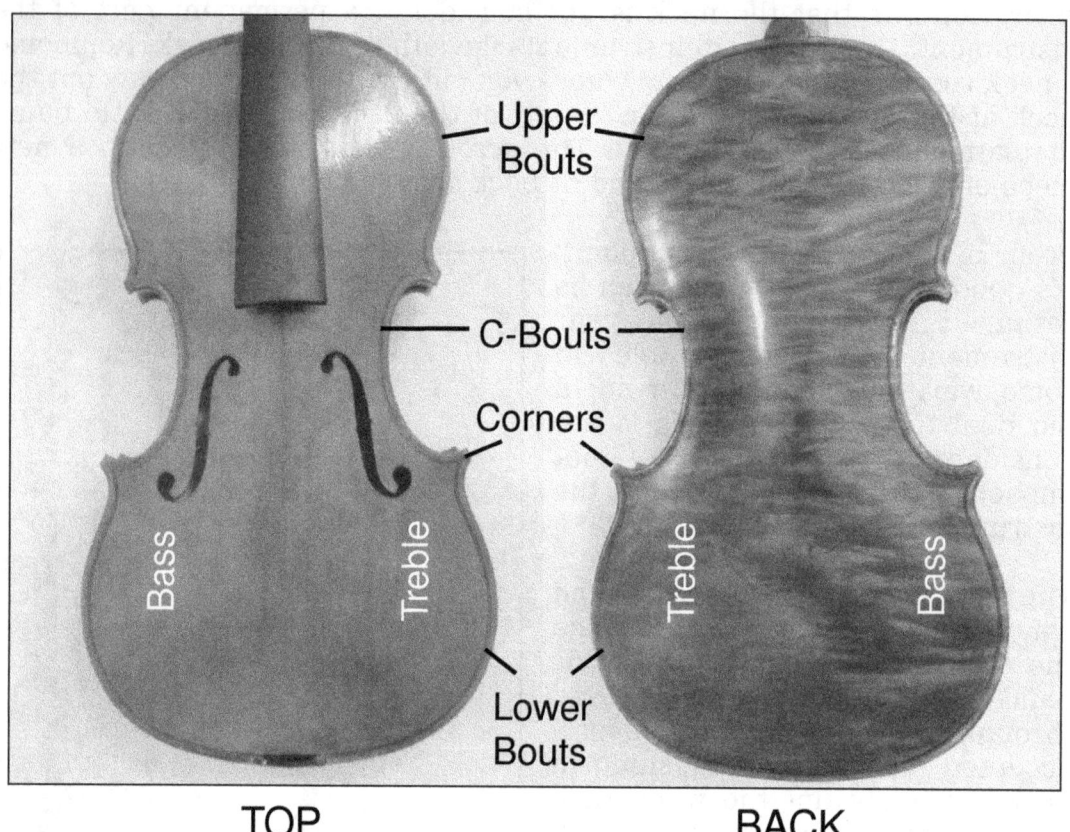

TOP   BACK

(Just a quick side note if you want to sound more knowledgeable about maple: The pretty stripes and waves that run horizontally across the back are referred to as "flame" or "figure." People often remark on the pretty "grain" on the maple, and the grain itself may indeed be nice in some way, but really what people are remarking on is the flame. Grain runs perpendicular to the flame.)

The basic sections of the body include upper-bouts, C-bouts, lower-bouts, and corners.

It's more helpful when talking about violins to use the terms "bass side" and "treble side" which are fixed, rather than "left" and "right." (Sort of like using "east" and "west" when giving directions, which aren't dependent on which way you're facing.) The entire left half of the instrument as the top is facing you (endbutton at the bottom) is the bass side. The right half is the treble. This reflects the pitches of the strings. If you flip the instrument over, the bass side is still the bass side, it's just now on the right as the back is facing you.

RIBS

The sides of the instrument are usually made of maple, and the technical term for them is "ribs." Ribs are also identified in terms of uppers, C's, and lowers, and describing them in terms of bass-side and treble-side is useful.

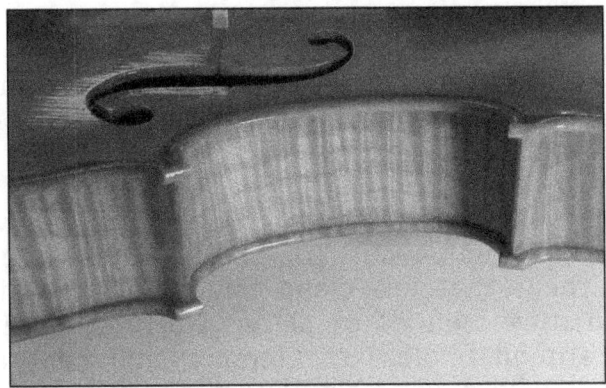

Ribs are purposely glued to the top and back with slightly weaker glue in order to provide the instrument a means of relieving tension in certain circumstances, usually related to weather's impact on the wood. Seams are designed to open if the instrument is under tension, because the instrument's other option for relieving that tension is to crack.

SHOULDERS

The ribs at the top of the instrument near the neck are referred to as shoulders. The shoulder on the treble side in particular can have problems with varnish wear, since that is a place players often rest their hand.

CRACKS vs OPEN SEAMS

This is an important distinction. A seam is anywhere two different pieces of wood are joined together with glue. A crack is when a single piece of wood is now broken.

If the instrument is opening up at a seam, where a rib meets a plate, that's usually a simple fix. There are also seams straight up the top of the instrument (which is nearly always made of two pieces glued together up the middle), and up the back if the maple is in two pieces. Those are referred to as "center seams." The center seam up the back is easy to see, but the center seam on the top is obscured by the fingerboard and tailpiece, so most people aren't aware of it. Those seams can come open too, and that's a bigger problem, but still different from an actual crack where a single piece of wood now needs to be repaired.

A crack is nearly always more complicated to fix than an open seam, so being able to recognize and articulate the difference is helpful when describing a problem to a luthier.

All cracks are not equal. Being able to articulate exactly where a crack is and what it looks like is important. Top cracks are often easily fixed, back cracks less so. Cracks that are clean and along a grain line are very different from puncture wounds or places were things are splintered or crushed. Cracks around f-holes are common and generally not hard to deal with. A crack where your soundpost sits can be the end for the average student violin. (We'll discuss soundposts in a few pages.)

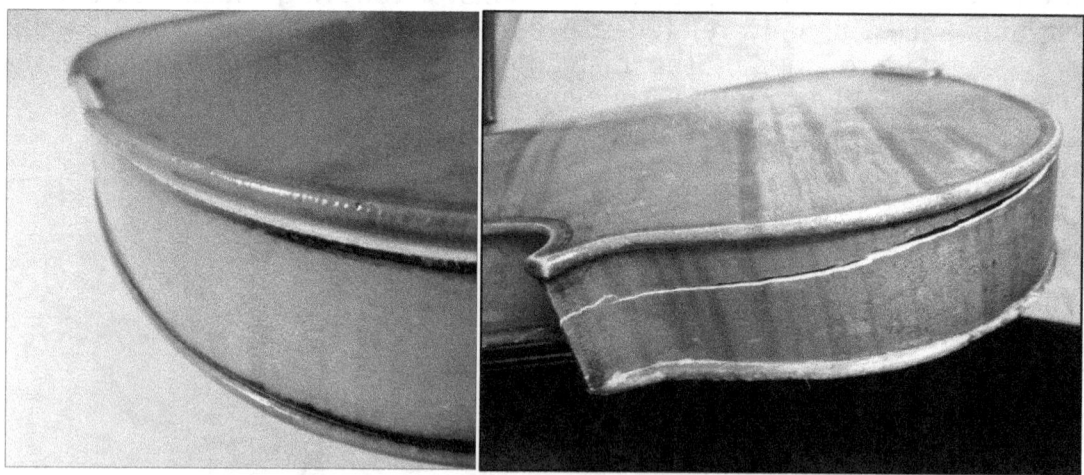

Open Seam   Rib Crack

F-HOLES

Parts of the f-hole include the upper-eye, stem, lower-eye, the wings, and the notches. F-hole cracks are common, so it can be good to be able to explain one specifically. (For instance, saying, "There is a crack on the bass-side f-hole from the lower-eye to the C-bout" provides a luthier with real information.)

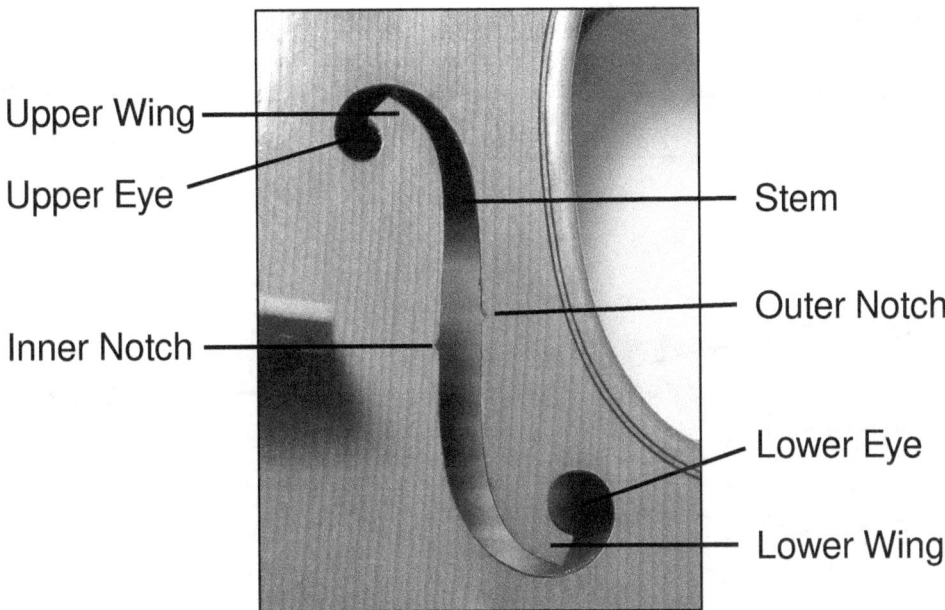

The inner notches on the f-hole, ideally, are there to help position the bridge. If you were to run a line across the top connecting the two notches, it should run through the middle of the bridge feet.

Some instruments are wonky and the notches don't line up where they should, so don't assume anything, but generally on typical student instruments if the bridge is way out of line with those notches, you can conclude it is in the wrong place. If you don't feel comfortable moving a bridge (especially on a nice instrument), take it to a luthier. We move bridges all day long and it only takes us a second.

BRIDGE

Bridges have weirdly corporeal sounding parts: The heart, chest, kidneys, ankles, and feet. Most people are surprised when they finally notice that bridges are not symmetrical—the curve on the top is lower on the treble side.

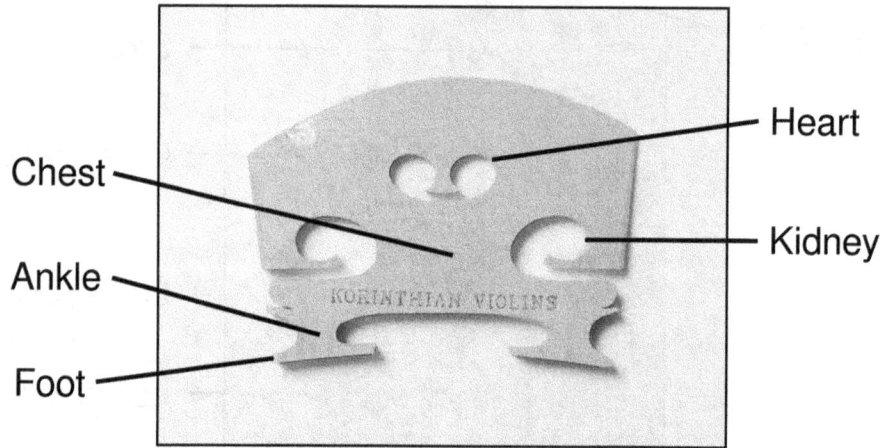

Bridges have string slots, and on the one for the highest treble string there is usually a "parchment" or "drum skin" attached as protection from the thinnest string slicing through the wood too quickly.

The first thing I wish more people knew about bridges is they are not glued down. They are held onto the top by tension from the strings. (Every once in a while I get a call from someone asking what kind of glue they should use when their bridge falls down. I love those calls, because I get to intercept a potential disaster. It's way better than the cases where people didn't call first.)

The second thing I wish more people knew, is that bridges are not some interchangeable piece we have lying around in a drawer that will take two seconds to switch out if you need a new one. They are planed and fitted and carved to work on one specific instrument in one particular spot.

A bridge blank may not look wildly different to the untrained eye from a finished bridge, but there are hours of work involved in cutting the bottoms of the feet to match a particular top, setting the string heights to match the fingerboard, and additional carving to make the bridge work correctly. It's the labor you are paying for when you buy a bridge, and highly-skilled labor at that.

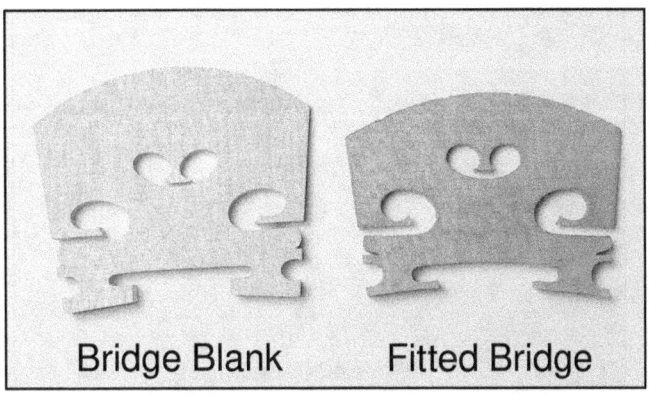
Bridge Blank   Fitted Bridge

AFTER-LENGTH

Related to the placement of the bridge is the after-length. The after-length is the segment of string that rests between the bridge and the tailpiece. It resonates, and has a surprisingly big impact on the overall sound of the instrument.

BRIDGE WARPING

It's important to know that bridges that have not been checked and adjusted properly can warp. Meaning they take on a new bent shape, usually leaning forward toward the fingerboard. Some get so bad that they look like they are doing the limbo, like this cello bridge that came across my bench one day. (The square sitting there shows how the bridge should be standing.)

I've seen many bridges that fall over frequently when they are warped, and more than a few that have snapped in half. If you think your bridge is warped, take it to a luthier. In many cases it can be straightened, but depending on how bad it is, it may need to be replaced. (There is more about how to identify if a bridge is warped in Chapter 2, as well as what to about them in Chapters 8 and 9.)

SOUNDPOST

While we are looking around in the area of the f-holes and the bridge, let's identify a few things inside the instrument. Most people are aware of the soundpost (or "post" for short), which you can see through the treble f-hole. It's a vertical dowel made of spruce, and it's positioned very specifically inside and behind the treble bridge foot. The main reason you can't just shove your bridge around wherever, is because it works in tandem with the soundpost, and the two things need to maintain a particular relationship to one another.

Soundposts are a structural element of a violin that need to be moved or replaced periodically. They are not glued in. They are held in place by tension, so if you loosen all your strings at once, you risk the post falling over or moving.

Soundposts stretch out the instrument over time. So when someone says your post needs to be replaced because it's too short, it's not that the post has changed, it's that the instrument has changed around it, and the existing post can't apply enough tension to do its job correctly anymore.

Beyond having a structural function, the placement and tension of the post fundamentally impacts the sound of your instrument and the way it performs. Soundpost adjustments are common. If your instrument is not responding the way it once did, take it to a luthier and ask about your post.

People often ask me how I get to the soundpost, many jumping to the conclusion I have to take the top off the instrument to move it. We actually reach the soundpost through the f-holes. As a result, you'll often see f-holes on the treble side of the instrument with chips or dings along the stem where people had a mishap with a soundpost setter. (Using a soundpost setter is a little like playing the game Operation.) Typical soundpost setters have a sharp end to stab the post in order to hold it, and a flared end designed to push and pull the post once it's standing inside the instrument.

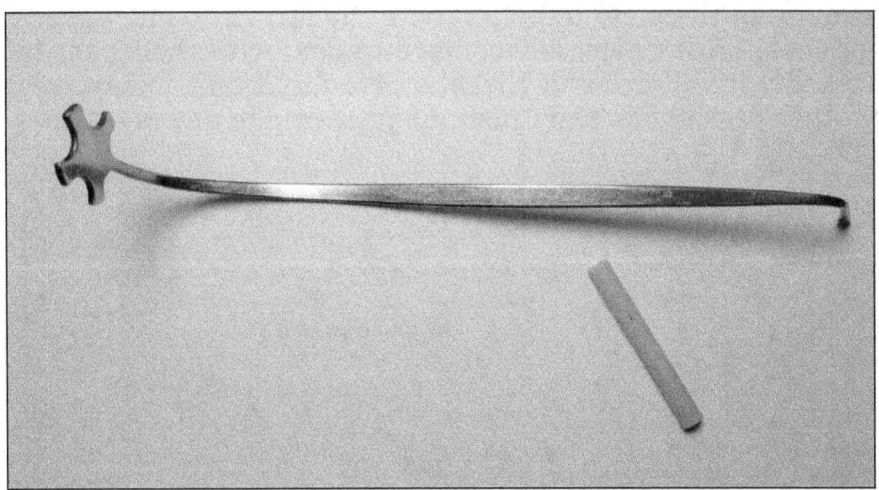

If your soundpost is rolling around inside your violin, loosen all the strings to take tension off the bridge, and take it to a luthier.

Don't mess with the soundpost yourself unless you have real training. I have met too many teachers who were misled by someone into believing that knocking around a post isn't that hard. Trust me, without a lot of

19

practice, it's hard. You can't see the straightness of a post from only the angle observable through the f-hole; you also need to sight it through the hole at the endbutton. This can't be done without taking tension off the whole instrument, which I would never advise a player or teacher to do.

When teachers who own soundpost setters move their students' posts, I worry about how they are measuring and tracking what they are doing. I understand the temptation to improve the sound of a student's instrument right away during a lesson. But there is a real possibility of creating a soundpost crack, where you damage the top or the back by putting the post in the wrong place. A soundpost crack on a cheap instrument is a death sentence for it in my book. A soundpost crack on a nice instrument is a long and expensive repair.

BASS BAR

On the other side of the bridge from the soundpost is the bass bar. You can see part of it through the upper-eye of the bass-side f-hole. Most people who come into my shop are unaware of the bass bar. It's a long structural element that runs roughly beneath your lowest string, and it couples more of the plate to help create the larger sound waves that make lower pitches. Most people never have to deal with their bass bar, but it's good to know it's there, and that it's also important in bridge placement (and another reason you can't just put your bridge any old place).

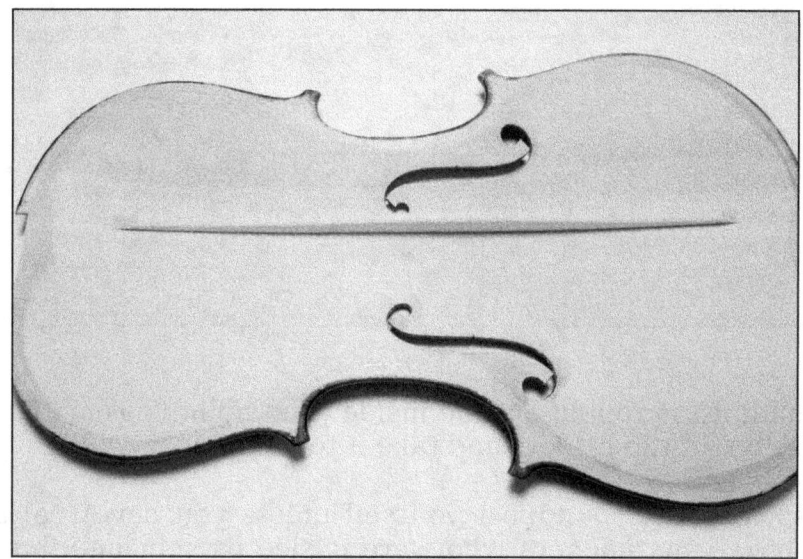

LININGS

Another thing inside your violin you may be unaware of are the linings. The ribs are too thin to provide enough surface area to glue the plates to, so there are additional pieces of light wood along the edges of the ribs to create more space for gluing.

Most people never have to deal with their linings, but they can cause problems if they come loose, and again, it's just good to know they exist.

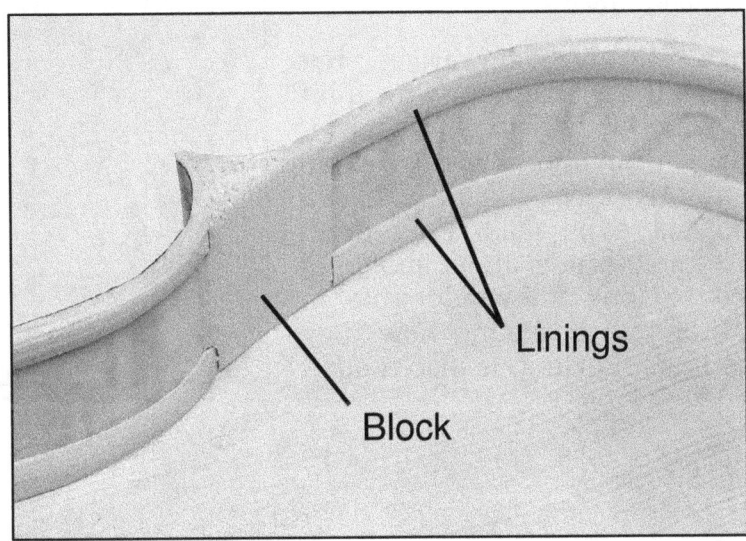

BLOCKS

There are six blocks inside a violin: One in each corner, one at the lower end, and one at the upper end which the neck is set into. Blocks are usually made of spruce or willow, and they are the structures that support the ribs, linings, and plates.

Common repair issues that involve the blocks would be if a rib starts to pull away from one, or if a plate seam opens at a block.

Scarier repairs involving blocks are if the neck is pulling out of the upper one, or if either of the endblocks become cracked or damaged and the instrument has to be opened to repair or replace them.

For most makers, blocks are the first part of the instrument we make. And they are a perfect introduction to violin building when you are a student, because they are a good lesson in making things flat, smooth, and square.

PURFLING

Purfling is the inlay that creates those little lines that run along the edges of the top and the back plates. Where the purfling meets in the corners, it ends in what we call a "bee sting." I think an especially pretty example of this is from that same Amati violin I showed at the beginning of this chapter.

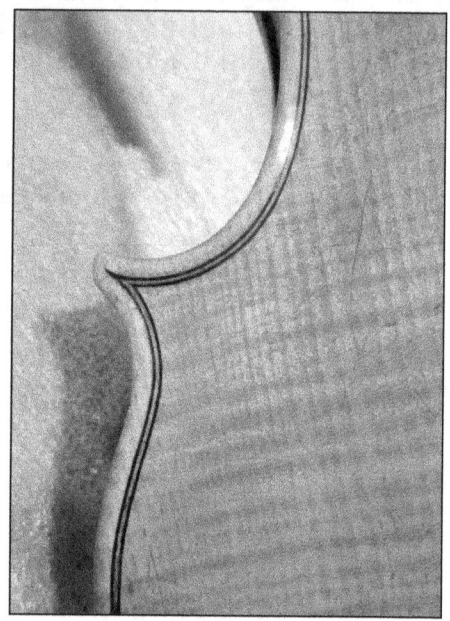

Purfling looks purely decorative, but actually provides the instrument with a bit of protection, which is why it's not great if yours is simply drawn on. Many cheap instruments merely have purfling drawn on, and often not even well. (You don't really need to know much about purfling, but it is nice to look knowledgeable in front of a luthier by not asking how they draw on those lines. Purfling is also a good Scrabble word.)

TAILPIECE

The tailpiece (or simply "tail") is the part that the ends of the strings are secured to at the lower end of the instrument. They can be made of wood, plastic, carbon fiber, or metal. They come in a variety of slightly different shapes and can be fancy or plain.

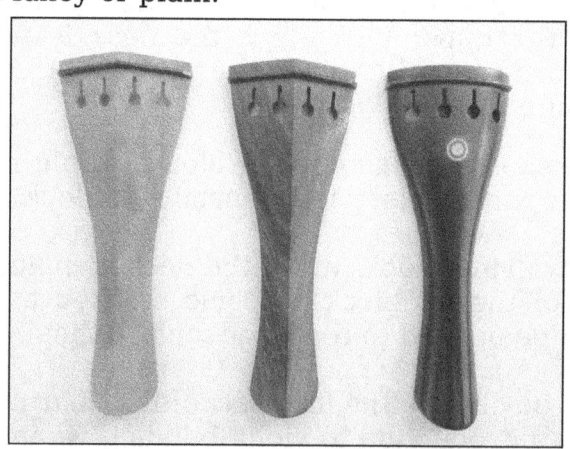

FINE TUNERS

Fine tuners are attached to tailpieces to assist players in making minute adjustments to the pitch of the strings. There are several different types, including Hill (or "hook"), post, Suzuki, among others. Instruments used by players who are skilled with their pegs tend to have only a single fine tuner on their highest-pitched string. A player with geared pegs that are capable of making fine adjustments by themselves may choose to have no fine tuners on their tailpiece at all.

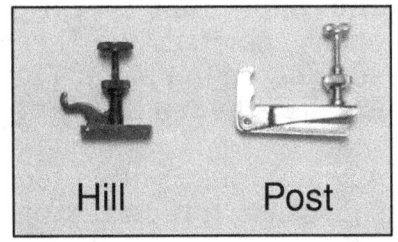
Hill   Post

Students usually need fine tuners on every string, and in that case I recommend they have them built right into the tailpiece, rather than have fine tuners added on. This is referred to as a Wittner, or Wittner-style tailpiece.

TAILGUT

The tailgut is the name for the string/filament/wire bit that is attached to the bottom of the tailpiece and loops around the end button.

The tailgut is what is generally holding everything together, so if the tailgut breaks, it can be quite traumatic for the player. Those calls are usually people in tears saying their violin just exploded. Thankfully it's an easy fix. For a luthier.

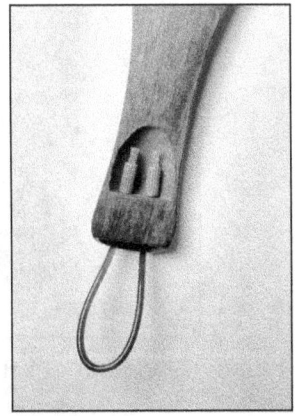

SADDLE

The tailgut runs over a piece of ebony inserted into the bottom edge of the top plate. That piece is called the saddle.

A saddle that is fitted too tightly can cause top cracks on either side of it. These are appropriately called "saddle cracks" and they are all too common. If you have a saddle crack, you need to take it to a luthier right away before it spreads far enough up the instrument that it becomes a bigger problem. Repairing a saddle crack involves removing the saddle and adjusting it so that it fits properly to prevent that crack from happening again.

CHINREST

The name "chinrest" is actually a misnomer, because it's really more of a place to rest your jaw. I see many people unnecessarily dealing with discomfort because the natural position of their jaw on the instrument does not align with the plate (or main surface) of the chinrest. More often than not, it's because they want to place their jaw partially over the tailpiece, and the plate of the chinrest is set completely to the left of it. Several styles of chinrest exist to solve this problem.

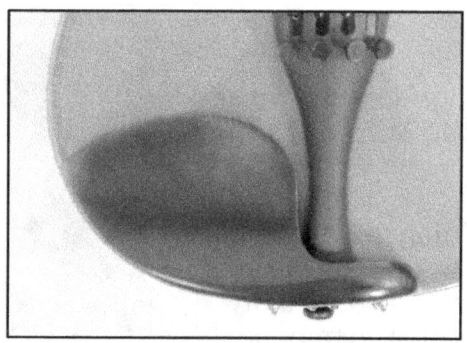
Guarneri

Teka

Sometimes better comfort is a matter of height, where a player needs a chinrest that is shorter or taller. Some players are better off with no chinrest at all (which is how these instruments were originally played). There are many kinds of chinrests. If you suspect your chinrest isn't a good match for you, talk to a luthier and look at other options.

I think the number one thing older players are surprised about if they only have experience with one instrument their whole lives, is how big a difference the right chinrest can make to their comfort and technique. About half the time people come to me thinking they need a different shoulder rest, they actually need a different chinrest (and vice versa), so it's a good thing to know to ask about if you are in a shop and can try things.

From a repair standpoint, the biggest issues with chinrests involve problems from over tightening them. Most chinrests use metal barrels with holes in them that you are supposed to insert a chinrest key into in order to turn them to adjust tightness. If whatever you are using as a key (most people resort to a paperclip) is too long, it's very easy to scratch up the ribs underneath the barrels.

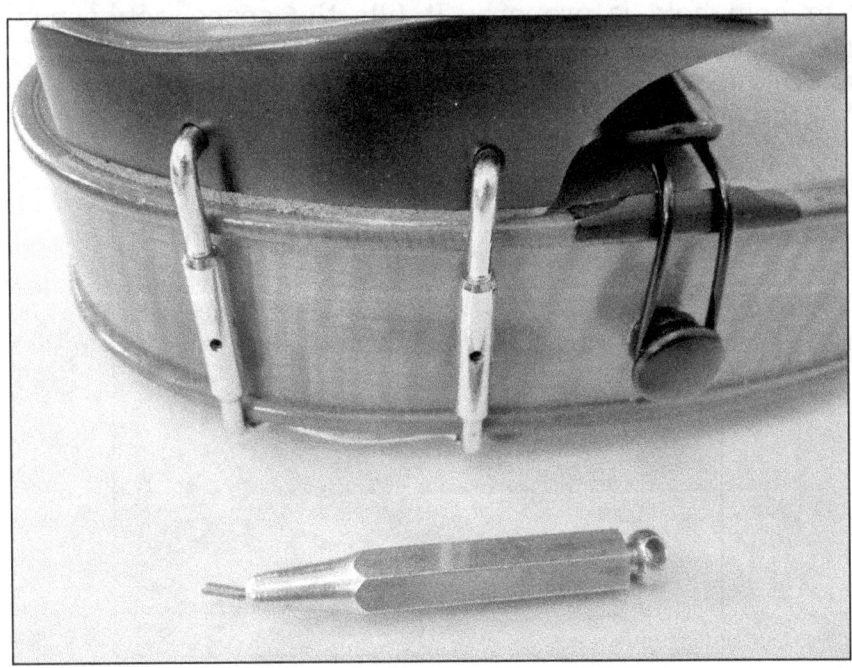

Make sure to alternate turns with the chinrest key from one barrel to the other. If the sides become imbalanced they get really awkward to work with.

I trust people to tighten and loosen their own chinrests, just be mindful. If your chinrest clamps to the left of the lower block, don't over tighten. There is no structural support past the lower block, and ribs are thin, so you can crush the ribs that way. The edges of the plates are often damaged by people shoving the brackets on the chinrest in too hard. There can also be varnish issues when you remove a chinrest and find imprinting in the place where it used to sit. This is common, and if putting a new chinrest on in a different spot exposes such a problem and it bothers you, take it to a luthier.

It's also good to be aware that it's not uncommon for players to have an allergic reaction to nickel, which is what most chinrests are bracketed to the instrument with. If a player develops a rash from chinrest hardware, you can either use a chinrest cover or a cloth, or replace the chinrest with a hypoallergenic brand that doesn't use nickel.

SHOULDER REST

A shoulder rest is a piece of equipment you attach to the back of a violin or viola to help hold it properly. It fills the space between a player's shoulder/chest and the instrument so it can be held parallel to the floor, and without squeezing the instrument with your shoulder or grabbing it too hard at the neck.

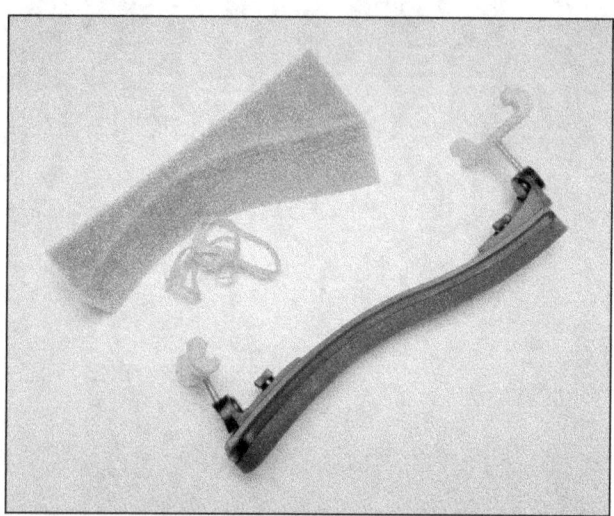

There are many kinds of shoulder rests because different people have different needs. Some players with short necks don't need a shoulder rest, or may simply use a cloth to protect their instrument. Some only need a simple makeup or kitchen sponge to add enough friction to keep the instrument from sliding off their shoulder. Many children use a contoured sponge specifically cut for use as a shoulder rest because it's less expensive than an adjustable one made from plastic or wood. Commercially available shoulder rests come in a wide variety of heights and shapes. Their composition can affect the sound of the instrument, since anything attached to it that vibrates creates sound.

As mentioned earlier, about half the time people come to me looking for a different shoulder rest, it turns out they need a different chinrest, and vice versa. The right chinrest/shoulder rest combination is one where you can hold an instrument in the correct position without strain or discomfort. For some people this takes time to find.

VARNISH

Violins are varnished, not painted. There exist instruments that are painted, but they are seldom taken seriously. Paint is opaque, varnish is transparent. When violins need to have varnish damage addressed, it's referred to as "retouch."

Avoid touching varnish, particularly on an instrument that isn't yours. When someone hands you a violin, the proper way to take it is to grab it by the neck, and the endbutton. (More about varnish in Chapter 4.)

IMPRINTING

Imprinting is when varnish picks up texture from something that presses into it. As mentioned earlier, that often happens where chinrests make contact with varnish because they are pressed into it so tightly. It can also happen in cases, usually on the back where the instrument is regularly pressed against fabric. It can happen from rubber bands or sponges left on too long, or places where shoulder rests touch the edges and back. Many times the bridge will leave "footprints" in a top where the varnish has been displaced from pressure.

There are violins with very soft varnish that imprint easily—in some cases even picking up fingerprints after having had years to dry—and others that never pick up an impression. Some of the softest varnish I've ever seen was on some very expensive instruments, so it is not considered a defect, although many people come to me assuming so.

In many instances, imprinting is a result of an instrument being exposed to heat (usually from being left in a hot car for hours). Imprinting is cosmetic, so not an emergency, but if you want it addressed, take it to a luthier.

ENDBUTTON

At the very bottom of the instrument is the endbutton. It fits into an internal structure called the lower block, and goes deeper into the instrument than I think most players realize. The endbutton shouldn't be bending any weird direction, or trying to slip out. Endbuttons can break, but it's rare. (The effect is the same as if the tailgut breaks, where everything comes apart.)

Moving on to the bow!

Of all the elements of the violin, the bow may carry the most misconceptions. At least, it did for me, before I began repairing them. I am not a bow maker. I worked for one for a while, and he taught me pretty much everything I know about bows, but I don't claim to know enough.

Let's start at the top:

TIP

The far end of the bow is the "tip" or the "head." The narrowest part of the stick is there, and is the most vulnerable to damage. The very topmost bit of the tip that comes to a snubbed point is the "nose."

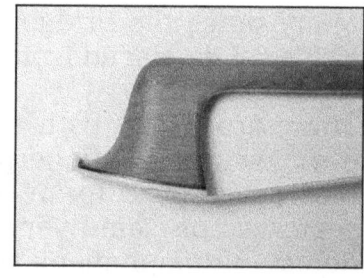

HEADPLATE

The piece on the front of the tip is called the headplate (or "faceplate"). Once upon a time it was made from ivory, but nowadays it's made from bone, or plastic (referred to loftily as "imitation ivory") if it's white, or some kind of metal such as nickel or silver.

The headplate plays an important role in protecting the entire tip. If yours is broken, take it to a luthier.

On a decent bow, there is a black piece called a "liner" between the headplate and the wood of the tip. On cheap fiberglass bows the headplate is just molded straight into the rest of the tip and there aren't separate parts.

MORTISES

A "mortise" is a fancy word for hole. The bow has one inside the tip, one inside the frog, and one in the stick at the frog end.

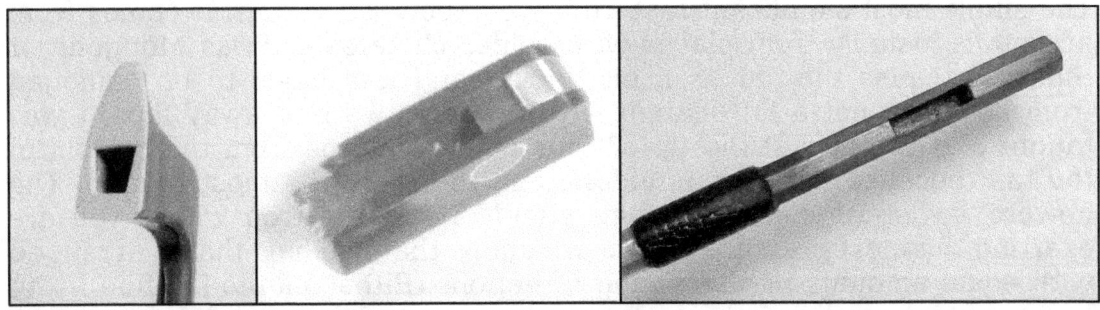

PLUGS

A typical bow has two plugs: One in the head, and one in the frog. They are usually made from wood, sometimes made from plastic, in rare cases made of lead. Their job is to hold in the hair at each end of the bow. Although on some inexpensive bows there might be a screw in the frog instead of a plug to secure the hair. Occasionally, someone leaves out the plug and uses a nail. (In those instances, I throw out the nail and carve a fresh plug.)

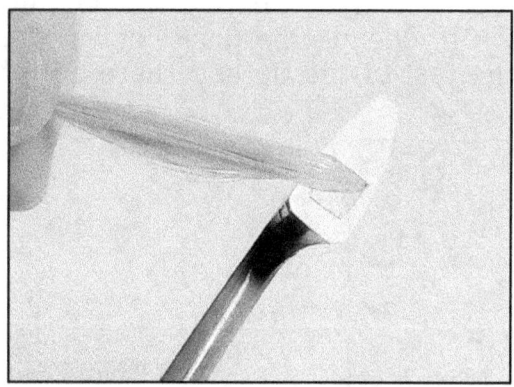 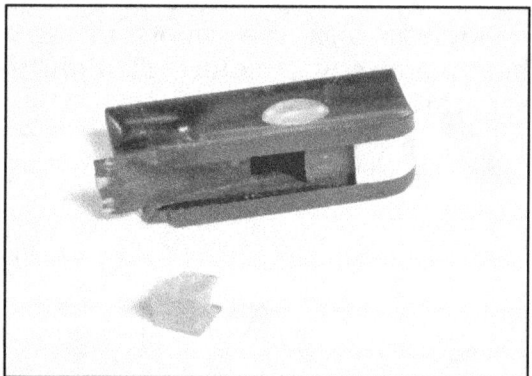

The cool thing about the plugs, is that they are cut to tapers that fit well enough in their respective mortises that they don't need any adhesive to hold everything in place. They simply balance there. You can reuse a well cut plug several times. (Unskilled people find endless ways to make poorly cut plugs stay, with everything from glue to sealing wax to dental compound. I hate it when I have to waste time digging out bad plugs from a bad previous rehair.)

HAIR

The single most significant feature of your bow is the hair. It comes from horsetails, usually from places with colder climates such as Mongolia or Siberia because the hair is a bit thicker and less likely to be damaged from having spent a lot of time on the horse swatting away flies. I was taught that the hair at the tip of your bow should be from the bottom of the tail (because that hair is oldest, and therefore the most brittle). The newest, strongest end of the hair should be at the frog where you are exerting the most pressure. There are shops that use hair that is arranged with equal amounts in alternating directions. Either method is fine if the hair is of high quality and your luthier knows what they are doing.

Don't touch the horsehair on your bow with your fingers. Don't let it come in contact with anything greasy, wet, or dirty.

REHAIR

A rehair is the term for replacing the horsehair on a bow. On average, this should be done annually. It's an important part of basic bow maintenance. This photo is of my basic rehair setup. (And yes, that's a small comb in the hair. Really no better way to work with hair than with a comb.)

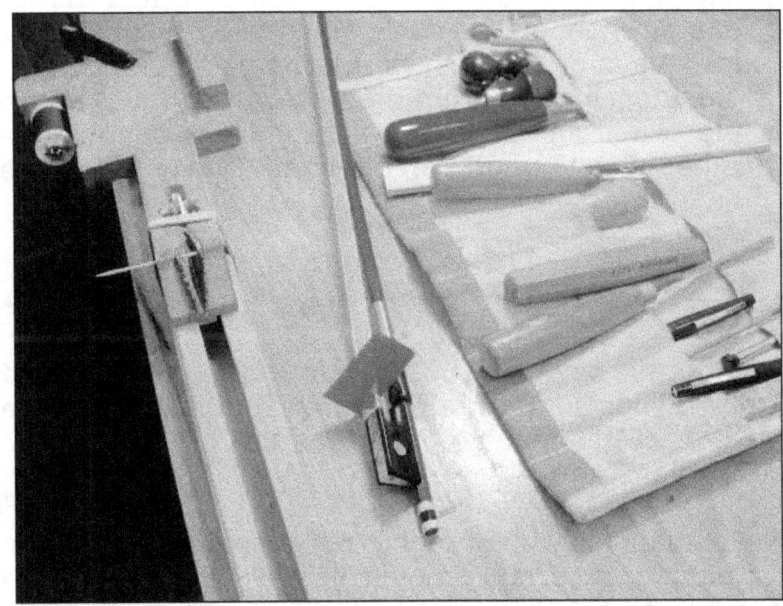

ROSIN

Rosin is a resin made from tree sap, and it's used to make bow hair sticky in order to make the strings vibrate. The hair is covered with small scales that hold the rosin when you rub it on. The stickiness of the rosin enables the hair to grab the strings. When you rub a rosined bow against a string, it has the effect of grabbing and releasing it as if you were plucking over and over, but incredibly fast. When all those scales eventually become stripped away from use, there is nothing for the rosin to cling to, and the bow ceases to grab effectively. I can usually tell someone needs a rehair by the excessive amount of rosin dust everywhere from a player's desperate attempts to make their bow hair work the way it used to.

STICK

The stick is usually made of pernambuco, but can also be made of brazilwood, carbon fiber, or a few other materials. It is either round or octagonal along its length. (Many players have beliefs about those shapes possessing different properties that I have never found to be true, but people are allowed to like what they like.)

CAMBER

An important element of the stick is its "camber." That's the name for the curve in the long direction of the stick. You should be able to tighten your bow to a nice playing tension without straightening out the stick completely. (Many teachers instruct their students to make sure their bow still has a "smile" when they tighten it.) If you can't, you may need to have the bow re-cambered so the bow can offer the proper resistance while you play.

WARPING

Warping is a different kind of bend to your stick, but one you don't want. If you sight down your stick from end to end, it should be straight when not under tension. If it's bending out to the left or right too much it may not be usable in that state.

Some people actually like a little bit of warping, depending on which direction it's leaning. A certain amount of warping can be corrected with a rehair if the luthier puts more tension on one side of the hair ribbon or the other. If a bow is too badly warped to use, often it can be straightened. Take it to a luthier.

WRAP

Moving down the stick, there is the wrap. The wrap is what it sounds like—something wrapped around the stick. It's there to protect the area where your fingers lie.

It can be metal, some kind of thread, or "whalebone." In the past, they used baleen from whales to create bow wraps, but today we use a plastic imitation, so if you see a bow that has those usually alternating black and light brown stripes for a wrap, you can refer to it as a "whale wrap" (or more precisely a "faux whalebone wrap") as opposed to a "silver wrap" (which is wire), or a "tinsel wrap" which is thinner and lighter.

Being able to say your "wrap is unwinding" is a helpful description. (Rather than saying your bow is falling apart, which is what many people tell me on the phone when their wrap is coming undone.)

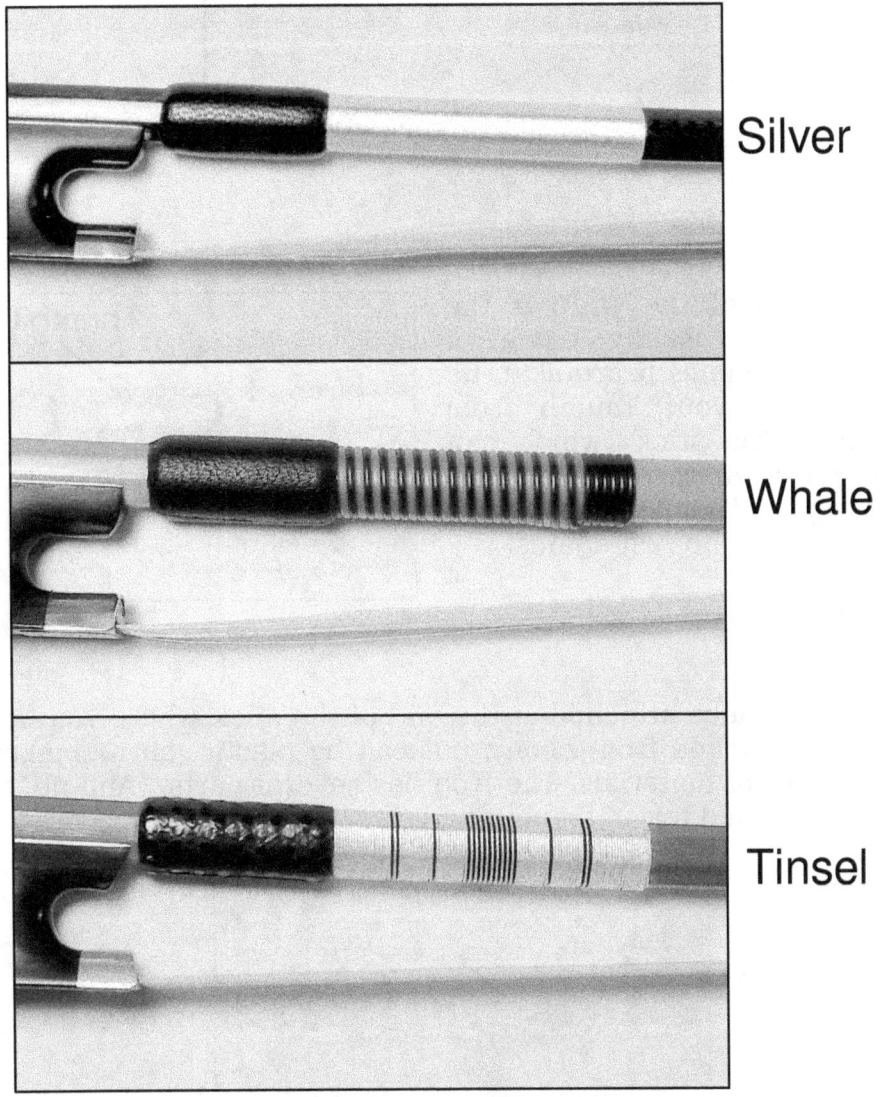

Some cheaper bows do not have a wrap, and simply use a long rubber piece as a wrap/grip combination instead.

COLLAR

Sometimes there is an extra piece of leather at the top of the wrap called a collar. Many times if a person's wrap is starting to come loose I can secure it with a collar.

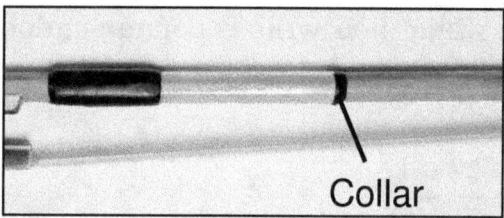
Collar

THUMB GRIP

At the frog end of the wrap is the thumb grip. It's usually made of leather, but sometimes lizard skin. Its job is to keep your thumb from wearing away the stick (which can happen if you wear through the grip and don't replace it), or simply to give your thumb a place to rest against.

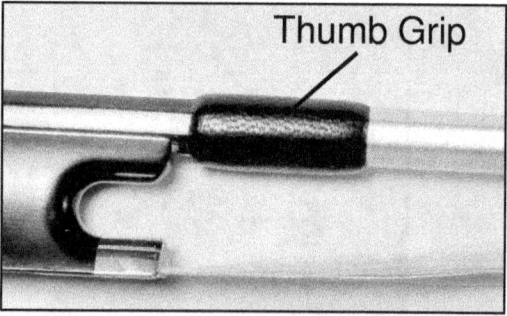
Thumb Grip

FROG

The frog is that piece attached at the end of the stick where you hold the bow. It's usually made from ebony, but can be plastic, horn, snakewood, and any number of materials. The frog has several parts. (And no, I don't know why it's named for an amphibian.)

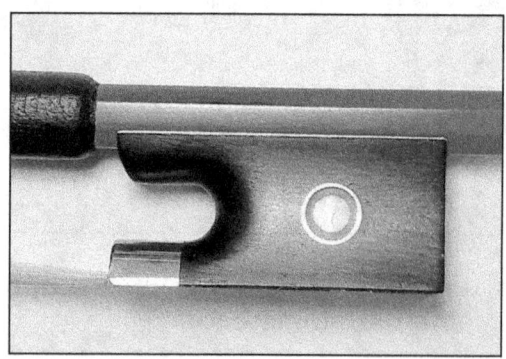

FERRULE

The metal ring with a flat side where the hair is coming out of the frog, is called the ferrule.

Teachers frequently come up with different words for it to teach their students, but I have only ever heard luthiers refer to it as the ferrule. It's best to have the real term if you want to be understood, and if ferrule is a new word to you, think of it as the wild part of your bow that is like a feral animal (since it's pronounced the same). If your ferrule comes loose, you need to take it to a luthier.

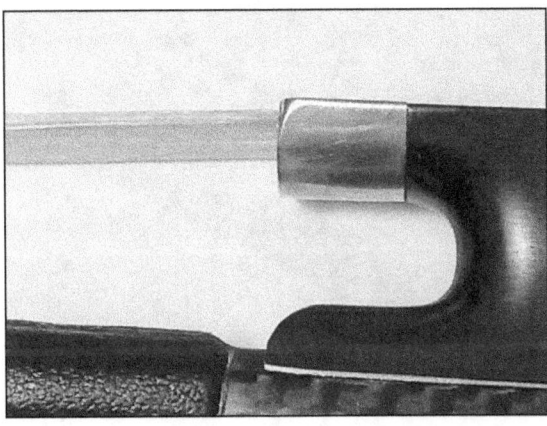

SPREAD WEDGE

Inside the ferrule is the spread wedge (or "spreading wedge"). It's that little piece of wood (or sometimes plastic) that's right up against the hair. It keeps the hair spread out at the frog end of the bow where the ribbon of hair is wider.

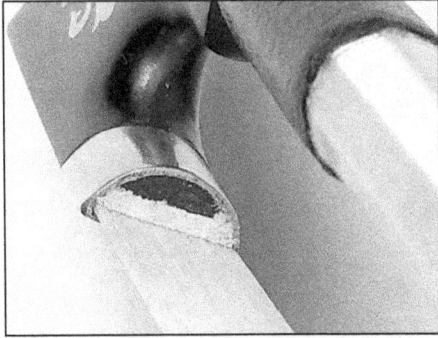

If your bow hair is all bunched up and sliding around at that end, you've lost your spread wedge and need to take it to a luthier.

SLIDE

The bulk of the surface of the flat, bottom part of the frog that butts up against the ferrule is the slide. It's often made of abalone or mother of pearl, but can also be made of plastic or carbon fiber.

Slides are often the prettiest part of a bow, but usually delicate. Inside the frog, under the slide, is the frog mortise and frog plug. If the slide is not sitting flush to the frog, something is wrong, and you should take it to a luthier.

SCREW and BUTTON

The bit that most people call the "screw" is actually called the "button."

I even have it labeled "screw" on my kid handout for convenience, because that's the way it functions and the way most people refer to it. But for repair purposes, it does help to be able to make a distinction. The button (the part you grasp) is attached to the screw, which is inside the stick.

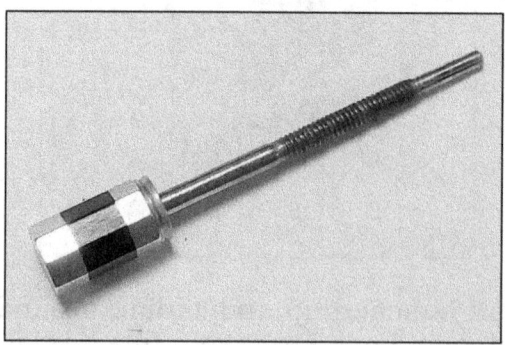

STICK MORTISE and EYELET

If you unscrew the button all the way and take the frog off the stick, you can see yet another mortise. The little brass piece on the frog that fits into that stick mortise (and that the screw actually screws into) is called the "eyelet."

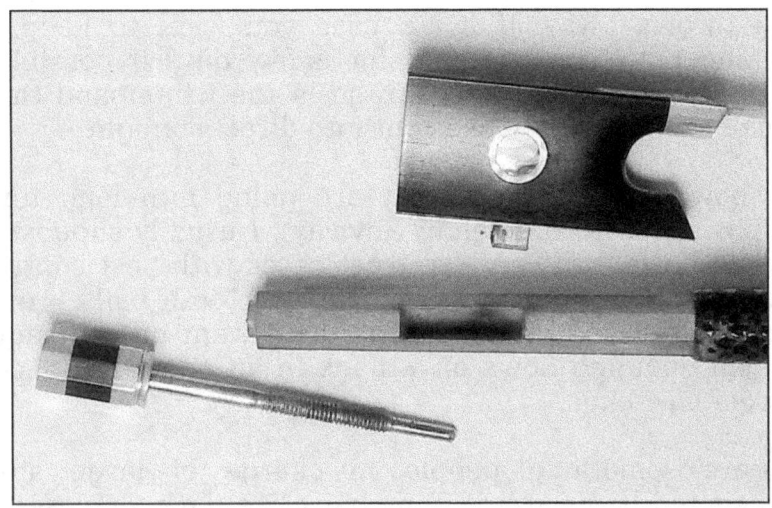

BOW BUGS

These are a thing. "Dermestid beetle" is the technical term, but they are insects that in larval form enjoy feasting on bow hair. They don't like sunlight, and they don't settle into cases that are handled regularly, so active players rarely encounter them. But bow bugs show up frequently in old cases that people have stored away in closets for years at a time. If you open an old case and the hair on the bow is falling apart in the middle, it's usually bow bugs. You can also come across small moltings as evidence they've been there. (That's what I see. I haven't come across live insects yet.)

In many circumstances, the case is usually old and unsafe or in disrepair and can be thrown away. If it's a case you want to keep, vacuum it thoroughly, and put it in a freezer for a few days if possible. (Here in Wisconsin I put cases out in the garage in the winter and that does the trick.) You can also put open cases out into direct sunlight.

To prevent bow bugs in cases that are going into long term storage (where the bows will need a rehair anyway), I usually suggest people cut the hair off old bows. You can also treat cases with pest control products designed for fabric, or cedar oils or satchels. Moth balls are not a good idea, because the poison they emit you don't want on your equipment. If you have room, hanging bows on a hook in an open, lit space will keep them safe from bow bugs.

Bow bugs are something people in charge of large stockpiles of instruments should be aware of. Bow bugs like dark, enclosed, neglected spaces, so keep bows sealed in plastic if they they won't be in use for a while, or hang them up out in the open if space allows.

Best defense against bow bugs: Practice! How's that for incentive? A scale a day keeps the bow bugs away.

There are, of course, many more terms to know if you want to dive deeper into luthier-land. But this much is a good working vocabulary for basic repair problems that can come up with a violin or bow. You are now ready to talk with clarity when entering a discussion with a luthier about what kind of help your violin needs should something go wrong.

CHAPTER 2

STRINGS 'N THINGS

This chapter is meant to primarily address questions about strings, but since everything on the violin is connected, I will also get into information about the pegs, tailpiece, bridge, and post.

CHOOSING STRINGS

There are many brands of strings. There are all kinds of new and improved strings coming out all the time. Teachers and players have endless opinions and preferences, and every instrument is different and will dictate its own needs. Therefore, I am not going to endorse one particular brand of string over another.

I will say that in most cases, when it comes to strings, you get what you pay for. If you're going to scrimp anywhere, it shouldn't be on strings. Cheap strings sound cheap, and life is too short to play on cheap strings if you don't absolutely have to. Strings are changed often enough that there is room to experiment. Ask your luthier for a recommendation if you need one. But this is a circumstance where bargain shopping may not be worth it. Counterfeit strings exist in abundance, and if a deal looks too good to be true, it probably is. Stick to reputable sources for buying your strings.

The windings on the ends of strings are color-coded. For strings I use often, I can tell at a glance what brand one is, and which pitch it's intended to be tuned to. If there is a brand of string you like and trust, get to know what they look like, and what the color coding for them is. It doesn't hurt to even notice details such as what the balls at the ends of them look like, since that's a place where makers of fake versions of strings often slip up.

And don't be afraid to mix different brands together. It's more common than not to like one kind of set for all but your highest string, and for that one use something else. Cellists in particular almost never use a full set of anything. Learn what sounds good on your particular instrument and for the kind of playing you do. However, if you find yourself trying to solve problems by using three or four different brands at a time on a single instrument, that's a good indicator you may have a setup issue that should be addressed. Take it to a luthier.

For students, I understand not wanting to spend too much, but it's still worth investing in a nice sounding string in order to make playing worthwhile. There are affordable, decent brands out there, I swear. It's worth it to do a little homework and ask around.

GENERAL STRING MAINTENANCE

Strings should be replaced on an instrument about once a year.

That varies a bit with the brand of string and the amount of playing you do, but as a rule of thumb, once a year is good. I know some professionals who change their strings every two to six weeks depending on what they are doing, and some students or casual players can get away with maybe two years out of a set of strings. But honestly, anything much past that is getting self-defeating.

I've met a lot of people who assume you only change strings when one breaks, which is not true. The real reason to change your strings is that the interiors of them deteriorate over time, and old strings sound dead. The windings on strings can also start to unravel or become nicked.

Wipe rosin off your strings and instrument whenever you are done playing. Use a dry, soft cloth. If you do this consistently, you should not have ungainly buildup happen. It is possible to clean your strings with a bit of alcohol or a very fine abrasive, but I don't advise it because both can damage your strings and shorten their life if done with any kind of frequency, so it's not a good habit to adopt.

For most players, it's a good idea to keep a spare set of strings in their case. There are two ways I recommend addressing the question of keeping spare strings: The first is to save your old set (assuming they aren't kinked or in some other way unusable) when you get a new set put on. Then the new set becomes the spare set the following year. The second is to keep a fresh set in your case, and put that on when you are ready for new strings, and get a new spare set.

Except for extra E strings, under normal circumstances players shouldn't need more than one spare set of strings in their case. Teachers may want to have more around, but even they should discard old strings if they've been sitting for more than a few years. (Some stores even have special recycling bins for old strings.)

Often when I put a new set of strings on someone's instrument, I give them the empty packaging stapled together and with the date on it. That way they know specifically what kinds of strings they have if they need to request or order more, and they can remember when they got their strings changed last. For many, that information is easy to forget, so a record of those details available in the case can be useful.

CHANGING STRINGS

Changing their own strings is something every player should learn to do correctly. I am always happy to install strings for people when they ask (mostly because that gives me an opportunity to check the instrument over in general and make sure nothing is wrong) but there are times when many players must do that on their own.

The first thing to know is to do them one at a time. The bridge is held in place by tension, so if you take off all your strings at once, the bridge will fall over, and possibly the post inside as well. I start with the lowest string and work my way across, but that's arbitrary. You can do them alphabetically if you feel like it, just do them one at a time.

If you happen to be stringing up an instrument where all the strings and the bridge are off, start with the outer two (G and E on violin, C and A on viola or cello), and then set the bridge up carefully underneath them. Bring those outer strings up to enough tension to hold the bridge in place, then fill in the remaining two strings.

While a string is off, that's a good moment to lubricate the string slots on both the nut and the bridge with graphite. Gently draw in the slots with a soft-lead pencil, and that will help the strings glide over those surfaces more smoothly. Do this liberally. It's an easy thing you can do yourself to make your strings and bridge function better.

 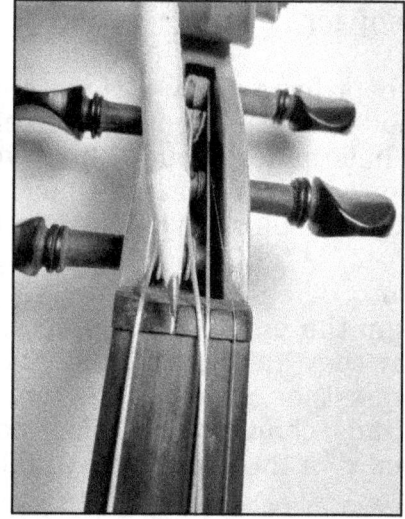

Start installation of each string at the tailpiece. The ball end slips into the available hole, and then the string slides up into the slot while the ball holds it from underneath.

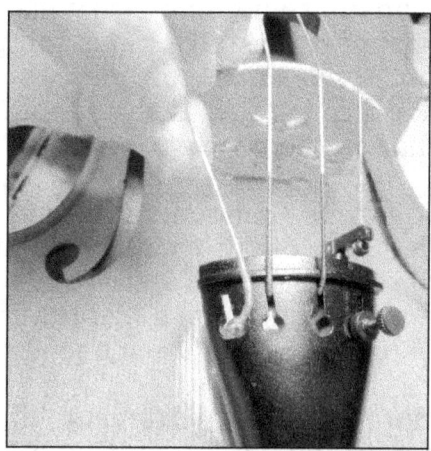

I see a lot of weird things where people try to wrap the string around the front end of the tailpiece and slip one end of the string through the hole in the ball, or somehow tie the strings in place, so don't do that. (There are instances using gut strings, particularly on period instruments, where tying is involved, but not on any of the instruments I regularly deal with, and certainly not on student violins.)

If for some reason the ball doesn't hold the string in place by simply catching along the underside of the tailpiece, something is wrong with the tailpiece. Take it to a luthier.

There are ball ends on all strings except for E strings, and viola A strings, where you have a choice between a ball or a loop end based on the fine tuner.

If you have a Wittner style tailpiece, you need a ball end. If you have a tailpiece with a single fine tuner for the highest string, you need to know if you have a post or a hook fine tuner before you buy strings for it.

If you have a "post" style fine tuner, it usually takes a ball end string, but often has a way to attach a loop as well. Post-style tuners are not really meant to hold something thicker than an E-string. Certain brands of string are also thicker than others. If a lower string doesn't fit between the two prongs, you can pry them a bit wider with a thin flat-head screwdriver. But be careful—those prongs break easily.

If you have a hook, or "Hill" style tuner, that takes a loop end. Although in a pinch you can sometimes turn a ball on its side and put the hook through the hole in the ball if it has one. (On occasion that can buzz, so it's not anyone's first choice.) You can also try removing a ball from the end of a string and convert it into a loop, but that's sometimes trickier than it sounds.

Once the string is installed in the tailpiece, run the string over the proper string slot on the bridge. It's hard to keep it there when the string is super loose, but keep an eye on it. You don't want the string pressing down into some other spot on the bridge as you start adding serious tension, because you will create unwanted extra grooves. (On student instruments, I see extra string grooves on both the bridge and the nut all the time, and they cause real confusion and problems, so be mindful not to create them.)

Next, put the other end of the string through the hole in the correct peg.

Pegs are not interchangeable. Each peg is fitted to its specific hole. It is unlikely your A peg will work in your G peg hole, for instance. Keep track of which peg goes where. This is another reason it's best to change one string at a time so you can't mix them up.

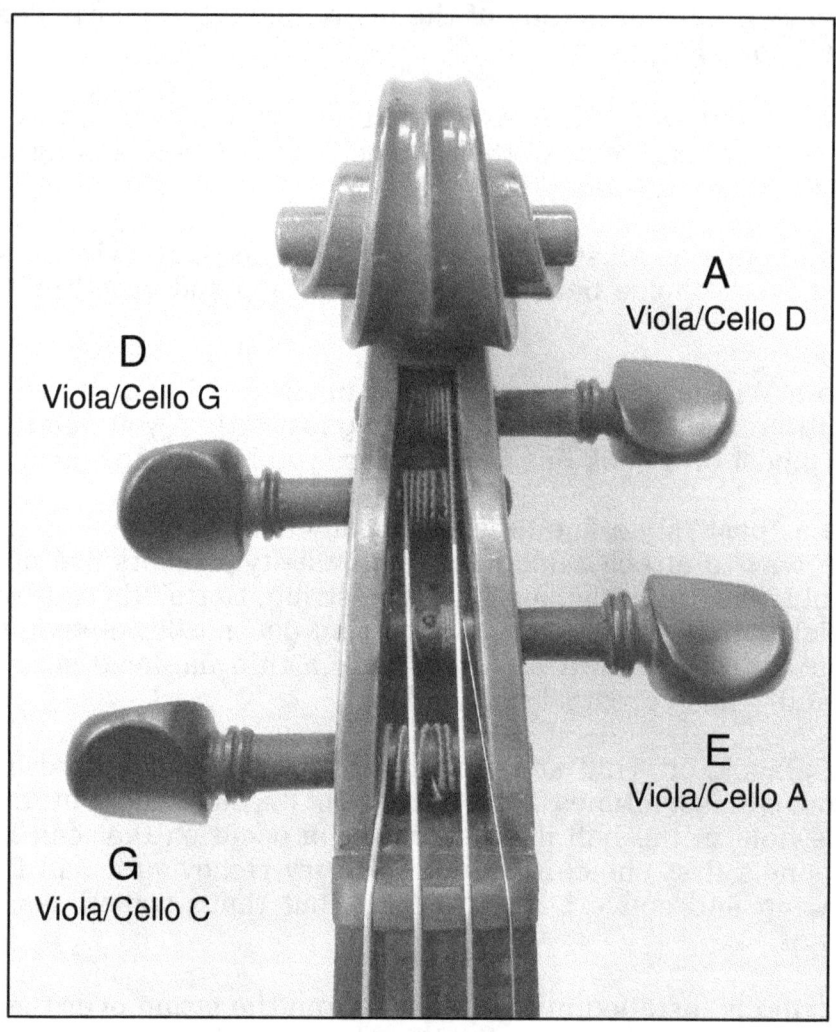

You want the tension on the strings to get tighter as you turn the peg away from you. (Meaning if you are looking straight at the peg head from the side view of the pegbox, you are turning it counter-clockwise to make the pitch go up on the bass-side, clockwise to do the same on the treble.) You want the string to be running over the top of the peg shaft, not underneath it.

Traditionally, violin pegs are "friction pegs." Pegs are tapered. The farther in you push a peg, the tighter it should get. But if your strings are wrapped on the pegs the right way, the strings will pull the pegs into the pegbox for you. You should not have to push often on a properly fitted and wound peg.

Put the end of the string through the string hole in the peg.

If the string hole in the peg is too close to the far end of the pegbox, or worse, in or past the pegbox wall, the hole will have to be re-drilled before you can proceed. (Jump ahead to PEGS SLIPPING.)

Ideally, it's good to do one wrap around the shaft at the narrow end, then move the string over toward the peg head and lay the string up against the box. The string should "track," meaning line up nicely with each previous turn, not randomly cross back and forth over itself. If the string is properly tracking up against the edge of the box, the peg should hold. If, when up to pitch, the peg feels too tight, back the string away from the pegbox wall. If it's too loose, track the string closer to the wall.

Don't worry about marring the finish inside the pegbox with the string. It's not a space where luthiers worry about varnish, and it's easy to retouch if necessary.

Make sure when you change strings that different ones aren't crossing over each other. I see this mistake most often with E strings on violin, because usually the string hole is easier to access on the wrong side of the A string. If the A string is in your way, you

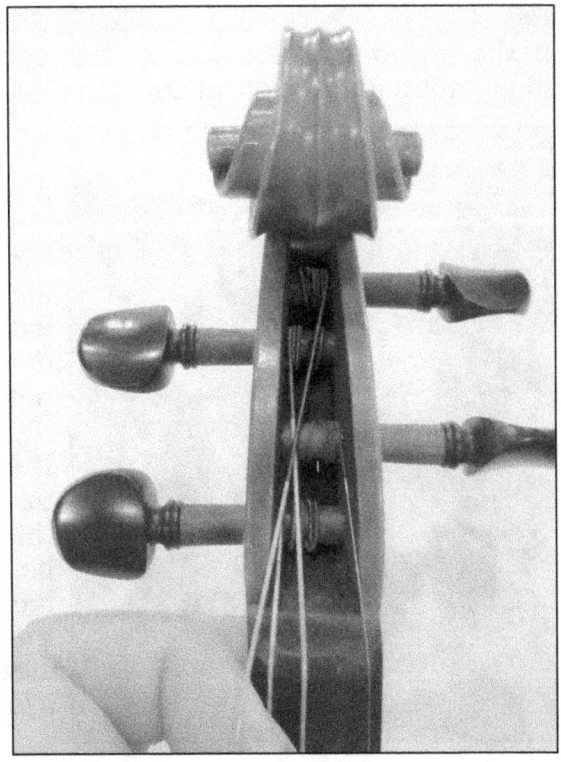

45

need to slide the E peg out enough to move the hole closer to the pegbox in order to insert the string, then push the peg back into place to continue winding. That, or loosen the A string enough to pull it temporarily out of your way.

Tune everything up to pitch slowly at first—a bit on each string, going back and forth among them in order to keep the overall tension somewhat even. Check that the bridge is standing straight frequently. (Explanation of how to do that appears later in this chapter.)

Strings need time to stretch out and adjust, so assume you will have to re-tune often the first few days. Unless there is something seriously wrong with your strings, it's not advisable to change them too close to a performance for just this reason. Many players prefer to have one to two weeks to break in their strings before a concert.

If you are having difficulty changing your strings, or getting them to tune properly, it's time to troubleshoot for various issues. Let's look at a few common ones:

STRING NOT STAYING IN THE PEG

If the string will not stay in the peg once you start turning it, there is likely not enough clearance at the bottom of the pegbox under that peg.

On poorly made instruments, there is often just enough room for a peg to fit across the box, but as soon as you add the thickness of a string wrapped around it to that equation, it doesn't work. You turn the peg, but the string can't go along as it gets caught on the bottom of the box.

If a string will not stay in a peg as you turn it, take the peg out and examine the bottom of the pegbox. You should be able to see where the string and peg have scraped at that area and confirm that inadequate peg and string clearance is the problem. This can usually be solved by carving extra room under the peg, but it can be tricky depending on the thickness left by the volute carved into the area behind the pegbox. DO NOT DO THIS YOURSELF. Take it to a luthier.

PEGS SLIPPING

More often than not, a tuning problem with the pegs has to do with how the strings are wound on. Most players are never taught how to do it properly, so that's understandable. If you wind your strings on the way I outlined, and your pegs are in decent working order, you shouldn't have this problem.

That said, you may need to adjust how the strings are wound as the weather changes. Here in Wisconsin, every October I get calls from people saying, "My pegs are broken! They all slip!" and every June I get calls from people saying, "My pegs are broken! They all stick!" The humidity, or lack thereof, changes how tight the pegs are going to feel. When the wood swells in the summer, the pegs stick, and then when it shrinks in the winter, the pegs slip. Simply re-track your strings properly onto the pegs again. That's an easy fix for anyone comfortable using friction pegs, and you don't need a luthier.

The next most common cause of a peg slipping, is when the string hole in the peg is in a bad spot.

The hole in the peg should be about a third of the way into the middle of the pegbox from the peg head side.

But pegs over time work their way across the box, and the holes move farther and farther toward the other side. Eventually, the hole can disappear inside that other wall and then tuning is not possible. At that point, there is no way for the peg to fit in far enough to stick, and you need a new hole. (I see this in school instruments all the time, and it's amazing how many little violins are suddenly tunable after just a few minutes with my drill.)

Here is the correct way to drill a new string hole:

First, mark where it will go. You want to drill the new hole perpendicular to the direction of the old hole in order not to weaken the shaft. Position the peg so you can see the old string hole clearly. Then turn the peg a quarter turn so you have a clear stretch of shaft to mark.

I mark the placement of the new hole with an awl. (Any good pokey tool will do.)

Then I remove the peg from the pegbox. This sounds obvious, but it's important enough to be worth stating. I've seen instruments where someone tried to re-drill a string hole in a peg *while it was still in the pegbox*, and they drilled right through the back of the volute. Remove the peg.

I use a 1/16" drill bit to make most string holes in pegs. You can go smaller for smaller strings if you have it, and of course go a bit larger for bigger strings, but I find 1/16" is sufficient for all violin and viola pegs. Always drill into a supporting piece of wood underneath so the exit hole doesn't splinter. I tend to run a mouse-tail file over the edges of the new holes to soften them slightly.

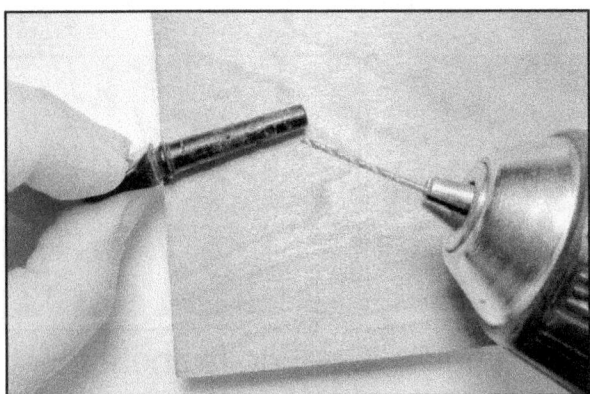
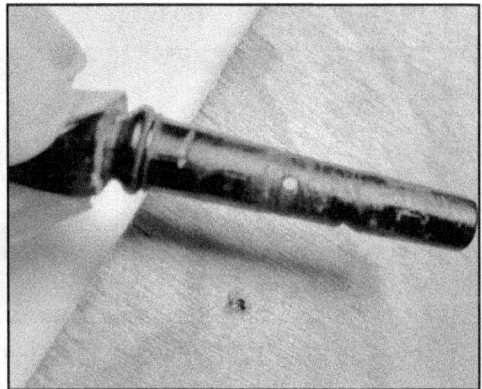

I will admit, I'm torn about whether this is something players should do themselves. It's not hard. I have taught teachers how to do this so they can do it for their students and am good with that. But for anyone not comfortable with a drill, this isn't the place to practice. Just because it's simple, doesn't mean someone can't mess it up. So as always, when in doubt, take it to a luthier.

For slipping pegs, I also see chalk as a solution that doesn't work the way people think it will. It often becomes glazed over time and makes things worse, even if initially it seems to do the trick. When I see chalk all over someone's pegs, I know to look for a variety of problems that the chalk cannot actually solve. Along the same lines, some people seek out peg dope for slipping pegs. I have never once used peg dope on a peg that was slipping too much. (Read ahead a little to learn about peg dope.)

Check the amount of usable shaft left on the pegs. Pegs work their way across the pegbox over time, and when the collar is essentially up against the pegbox, there is nothing thick enough left to hold the peg in place. You need a new peg, or possibly a pegbox bushing. (See pegbox bushing, page 9.) Take it to a luthier.

  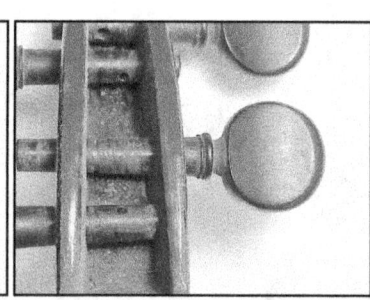

Healthy amount of peg shaft   Adequate amount of peg shaft   Peg is about to become un-tunable

If you are having problems with your pegs slipping, and it's not the way the strings are wound, and it's not the placement of the string hole in the peg, and you have enough peg shaft to work with, then more serious adjustments need to happen.

The holes in the pegbox itself probably need to be re-reamed, or the shafts of the pegs re-shaved, because something has become oval instead of round, or the two tapers don't match. Those things require specialized tools and a skilled touch. Take it to a luthier.

If your pegs are slipping, and you start getting too aggressive, beware of cracking the pegbox.

It is always a bad idea to just keep forcing a peg into the pegbox. Especially the top one (A for violin, D for viola) since it can cause a crack and lead to big problems. The most vulnerable spot on a scroll is where that peg is pressing into the top part of the pegbox wall. The grain runs that short direction, and if that area is too thin, and someone tries to force a badly fit peg too hard, that area can crack, and in some cases pop the whole scroll off.

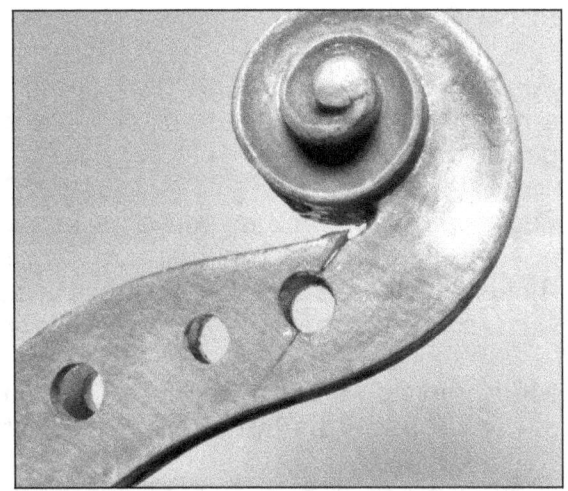

If you find yourself forcing any of your pegs too hard (after checking that the string winding and string hole in the peg are fine), take it to a luthier.

If you start to see cracking in the pegbox by that upper hole (or anywhere, really), take it to a luthier.

If you see a full-blown crack, take it to a luthier.

If the scroll pops off, take it to a luthier.

There is no do-it-yourself fix for any of this without endangering your instrument. (Take it to a luthier.)

PEGS STICKING

The first thing I said earlier about pegs slipping applies here, too: Most of the time when a peg is functional but not working, the string is wound on improperly. Pegs stick in the summer when it's hot and humid. Back the string up a bit farther away from the pegbox wall and it should work fine.

Short of someone maybe gluing pegs in place (and I did hear a story once about a well-meaning dad who thought he was doing his kid a favor by permanently keeping the strings "in tune" that way), I only see pegs stick because of wood swelling. Sometimes they can be impossibly stuck and I have to go at them with pliers. That's a procedure where I wrap the peg head with leather and gently but firmly pry the peg loose. This is something a player is welcome to try if they are exceedingly cautious. It's very easy to twist off the head of the peg and break it this way. Then a luthier has to drill out the broken peg shaft. Probably best to take it to a luthier before it reaches that point anyway.

If the peg is still a bit sticky after rewinding the string the correct way, you may need a bit of peg dope. (What's peg dope? Turn the page.)

PEG DOPE

Peg dope is a compound that comes in a little tube like lipstick, and is applied to the peg shaft in the places where it makes contact with the pegbox holes.

Peg dope is a combination of a lubricant with a fine grit for friction. On new peg holes, I often heat up peg dope a little in order to better coat those surfaces. Peg dope is more a means of treating the holes the pegs turn in, rather than the pegs themselves.

I like peg dope. I use peg dope. I would never send a new instrument out of my shop that hadn't been properly treated with peg dope.

However, peg dope is not magical.

Too many people expect peg dope to do all the things. Some people buy it to stop their pegs from slipping, or to make their pegs slip more, or to stop it from turning in an odd jumpy fashion. If your pegs aren't fitted properly, peg dope can't solve that. I see badly fit pegs slathered in excessive peg dope way too often, to the point where I don't sell peg dope to individual players. I'd rather examine the pegs and put any necessary peg dope on myself for free than have people misapplying it. (The important exception here is teachers in school programs, which you can read about in Chapter 8.)

When I change strings for people, I may apply a bit of peg dope if I think it will help the pegs move better. Good pegs don't need it every time. The average player should never come close to needing enough peg dope to necessitate owning a stick of it, so if you find yourself thinking peg dope will fix something drastic, take your instrument to a luthier. Because most likely something is wrong with the fit of the pegs, not their amount of lubrication.

GEARED PEGS

If all of that peg work sounds like too much trouble, there does exist a variety of decent geared pegs. The shafts are fixed in place in the pegbox holes, and there are gears hidden in the peg head that turn the string like a fine tuner.

I used to be rather biased against them except for people with pain issues in their hands, but the geared pegs on the market today have gotten quite nice. There are several that even have wooden heads that to the average person are aesthetically indistinguishable from traditional friction pegs. And there are even examples of antique instruments having geared pegs installed to save wear and tear on a fragile pegbox.

The instruction about winding strings up against the wall of the pegbox does not apply to geared pegs. Since the shafts are intended to remain in place, tracking the strings against the wall of the box could dislodge the pegs if they aren't secured well enough. Just keep the strings wound neatly in the middle of the shaft.

My only caveat about geared pegs is that I still believe students should learn to tune with traditional pegs first. It's a skill like any other on the violin, and one they should develop a comfort level with early.

TAILGUT FAILURE

If the pitch of the strings keeps dropping when you try to tune them, but the pegs aren't moving, and you keep hearing a small creaking sound each time the strings slip out of tune again, that means your tailgut is starting to go.

Stop everything and take it to a luthier.

Because when your tailgut completely goes, it sounds like a bomb going off, and it looks like the violin blew up. The tailpiece becomes disconnected from the endbutton, the bridge falls down, the strings go all over the place, and sometimes for added drama the soundpost starts rolling around inside the violin.

A typical tailgut is held in place by two small nuts that are screwed into place on the underside of the tailpiece. If the threading on the tailgut is defective and can't hold the nuts, they start to slide off in fits and starts. Unfortunately this only happens when the tailgut is under tension, so there is no good way to test it before you put it on an instrument. I've sent out more than one instrument with a faulty tailgut, and I'm grateful when people recognize there's a problem before it gets too far and I can replace it.

But the first clue to tailgut failure is all the strings abruptly going flat during tuning, so it's a good thing to know.

STRINGS BREAKING

With the exception of violin E's (because they are so thin), it's unusual to break a string. Unless the string is defective, the only time I see people breaking strings is when beginners try to tune their instrument the first time without supervision. (Then they learn their lesson and discover the fine tuners.)

The main thing to know when you are learning to use your pegs to tune is to aim below the pitch you want, and go up. Going above the intended pitch is when you risk breaking the string.

It can also happen if you put the wrong string on the wrong peg. The different strings are designed to be tightened to different lengths and tensions, so if you put a lower tension string on a peg intended for one with higher tension, and you try to bring it up to pitch, it will snap. (The higher pitched string on a low tension peg will sound floppy.) So always check the color codings on your strings before installing them.

If you are having problems with a particular string breaking repeatedly, the first thing to determine is at which end it is happening. If there is a specific problem on your instrument causing strings to break, it's happening at one end or the other.

If the string is breaking at the nut end every time, there may be a problem with the nut that needs to be filed. Take it to a luthier.

If the string is breaking at the fine tuner, you probably have a Hill style tuner and the hook is cutting through the loop. When they stamp those hooks out at the factory, one side ends up sharp. Either a luthier can file that side of the hook down to smooth it out, or they can place a protective cover over the hook. If you're changing your own strings, make sure to keep an eye out for that little protector if you have one. It's very small and easy to lose.

If you are breaking strings randomly at either end, either you got a bad batch of strings, or it's you, in which case you should not be putting on your own strings until you get some further instruction about tuning. Take it to a luthier.

STRING HEIGHTS

On fretted instruments people call this "action," but in violin-land we refer to "string heights." String heights are measured in metric. Nearly all violin work is measured in metric.

String heights are measured from the playing surface of the fingerboard, to the middle of the thickness of the string. The numbers I was taught to use for a new violin bridge are 5.5mm for the G, and 3.5mm for the E. (For viola: 6.5mm for the C, and 4mm for the A. For cello: 8.5mm for the C, and 5.5mm for the A.) There is a little bit of wiggle room there depending on the circumstances, but generally if your string heights get to be a millimeter too low, the whole bridge is too low, which can cause buzzing and other issues.

I don't expect any non-luthier to be able to accurately measure their own string heights, but they should be aware that string heights can change over time as instruments settle and weather conditions affect the wood. In my experience, most new instruments in their first year need to have their bridges cut down at least once. It takes an instrument some time to adjust to the tension on the neck from the strings, and they essentially pull the front end of the fingerboard down, which changes its relationship to the bridge. This is normal, and not some factory flaw.

If pressing down on the strings seems too hard, especially as you get closer to the bridge, take it to a luthier and get the bridge cut down.

CHECKING IF YOUR BRIDGE IS STANDING STRAIGHT

The only real danger in changing your own strings, is in not paying attention to the bridge while you do it.

In the previous chapter on vocabulary, I talked a little about bridges and how they can warp, but I'd like to explain that better here. The reason bridges warp (aside from if they are made of maple of inadequate quality), is that if they start to lean (usually forward, meaning toward the fingerboard) and no one stands them back up properly, the pressure of the strings can begin to crush them, and they become more and more bent over time.

The back of the bridge (the side facing the tailpiece) is essentially flat, and the front (the side facing the fingerboard) is rounded. That's part of how it withstands so much pressure from the strings—it's engineered a bit like an egg and can withstand a lot of force. But only if it's standing properly. The back of the bridge should be standing perpendicular to the top.

Only up to half of the diameter of your string should be embedded in the top of the bridge. If the string slots get too deep, instead of gliding over the top of the bridge, the strings start to drag the top of the bridge with them. Which means whenever you tighten your strings, you may be pulling the top of the bridge forward. If you suspect your strings slots are too deep, take it to a luthier.

The most likely time for the top of your bridge to get pulled out of place is when you change strings, because that's a lot of disruption at once. Also, as the strings stretch out, you need to keep tuning more frequently than normal.

After you put on each new string, you need to stop and check the bridge to see if it's leaning. After you tune most of the instrument up to pitch, you need to stop and check the bridge to see if it's leaning. Once you have finished tuning the instrument up to pitch, you need to stop and check the bridge to see if it's leaning again. Am I sounding naggy? Good. Because it's important. You need to be diligent about checking bridge straightness often while changing strings or the bridge can fall over with a bang, or even break.

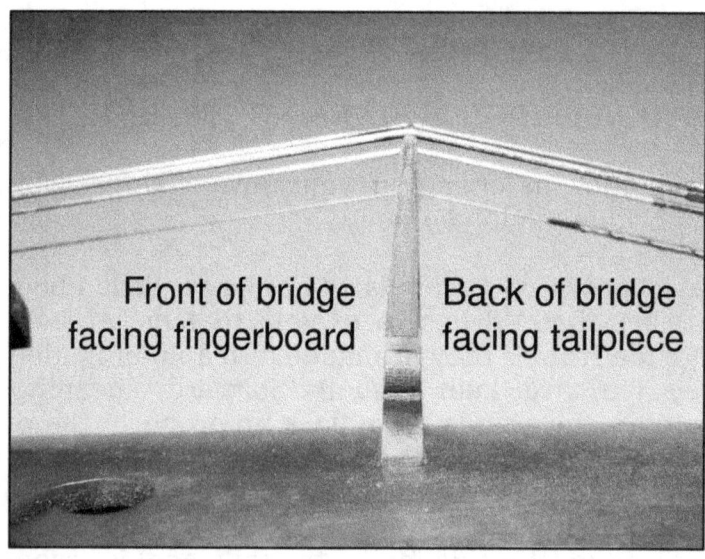

Here is how to check if a bridge is standing straight:

You sight the bridge from the bass side. Not the treble. Your bridge is not symmetrical, because the string height on the lowest tuned string is higher than on the treble side. The treble side of a bridge looks distorted and is harder to gauge by eye. So look at your bridge from the side view, G (or C) string toward you.

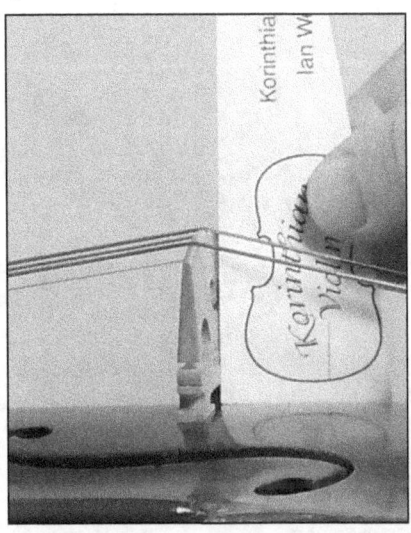

The back of the bridge should be perpendicular to the top. You can check this with a handy dandy business card (trimmed to fit if necessary), or just find a right angle in the background to compare against. The back of the bridge is essentially flat. The feet should sit flat against the top without gaps.

If your bridge is leaning forward, you can stand it back up yourself. If that makes you nervous, take it to a luthier. I stand up bridges that are leaning all day long. It only takes me a second. But if you want to, here's how I teach people to do it themselves:

Put your instrument firmly on your lap, bass side toward you (scroll to your left). Place your left hand over the instrument and settle it on the upper bout, fingers grasping over the edge onto the ribs. Do the same with your right hand over the lower bout. (In the chapter on varnish, I tell you never to touch the varnish, but this is an exception. This is varnish fulfilling its protective function and you have my permission in this case to manhandle it all you like.)

It's important to keep your hands firmly on the instrument like this, because as soon as your hands start to float above everything, you could lose control very easily and do something you will regret.

Once you have the instrument firmly grasped in your hands on your lap, meet your thumbs together on either side of the top of the bridge in the middle (between the D and A on violin, and the G and D on viola). If your hands are planted in place, and you press your thumbs into each other, it is hard to push the bridge too far and make a mistake. You only want to nudge it a millimeter or two. The feet should not move. (If the feet move out of place, and it's a nice instrument, take it to a luthier. If it's a weird little student instrument, just make sure the feet are lined up between the f-hole notches and that it's centered on the fingerboard.)

Push the top of the bridge the direction you want with your thumbs, sight the bridge again, check it against a business card if you like, and repeat as needed until you like how the bridge is standing.

If when you stand your bridge up it looks straight, but the feet aren't touching completely anymore, then your bridge is warped. Take it to a luthier. Often a bridge can be straightened, but in certain cases it makes more sense to replace it.

A FEW EXTRA NOTES ABOUT BRIDGES

In addition to standing straight, there are other things to know about the bridge:

It needs a proper curve along the top of it so you can pivot to different strings correctly with your bow. If a player can't stay on one string at a time and it doesn't seem to be a technique issue, have a luthier check that curve. (Some fiddle players opt for a flatter bridge profile to intentionally make it easier to hit other strings.)

The string spacing along that top edge curve needs to be even, and a particular width-span.

The bridge needs to be placed in a particular spot on the top (centered, and usually lined up with the f-hole notches—More on this in Chapter 8).

The feet need to fit (so they are in full contact with the top and that they don't slip).

It's important to mention that old or quirky instruments can be odd in terms of how their bridge stands or where it works best, and parts of the descriptions I've given may not exactly apply. Such instruments should definitely be checked by a luthier. For the average student instrument, however, teachers should be able to position and check bridges using the guidelines in this book.

A BIT ABOUT YOUR SOUNDPOST

The reason I'm taking a moment to talk about soundposts in the middle of a chapter about strings, is that the post has a profound effect on how the strings perform.

The placement of the soundpost in relation to your bridge is important to how your strings play and respond. The soundpost sits inside the treble bridge foot and behind it a bit. If it's sitting directly under the bridge, or noticeably far from it, it's wrong and needs to be addressed.

When someone needs a post adjustment, it usually means their instrument isn't responding as well as it should or once did. The strings aren't reacting quickly enough, or they sound unbalanced. There is small range of places to move the post to try to improve those things.

When most people come in asking for a soundpost adjustment I require them to stay as I do it, and determine for themselves when they like their sound best. In cases where it's a student instrument and the post is visibly leaning or standing in a strange spot, I can usually just determine a good placement myself and that works for the player. If I can't get a post to stand in the optimal spot because the instrument has stretched out too much over time, or if the post is badly fitted or not doing it's job right, I'll cut a new one.

STRING SPACING AT THE NUT

At the nut end in particular, teachers need to watch out for proper string spacing. On really cheap instruments, the string spacing can be uneven or too narrow, which can make playing difficult if not impossible. Before assuming a student isn't working hard enough at holding their fingers the right way to bridge over adjacent strings, make sure they actually have the space available to do it. You'd be shocked at the number of times that's the real problem.

Is there more that can go wrong with strings? Of course. Otherwise my job wouldn't stay interesting, I suppose. Just remember that when gathering information to decide what to do in your particular circumstance, it never hurts to get the opinion of a luthier as well.

And the only thing that comes to mind as a way to wrap up a chapter on strings, is with the old joke: "String players spend half their lives tuning, and half their lives playing out of tune." Get your pegs checked and prove 'em wrong!

CHAPTER 3

GLUE

This is a short chapter just to say: Whatever glue you have at home that you may want to use on your violin?

Don't.

Unless you have a pot of cooked hide glue and know how to adjust its strength for different applications (in which case you are already a trained luthier), keep your glue in the bottle.

Luthiers glue nearly everything with hide glue. Hide glue is exactly what it sounds like: Glue made from animal hides. (I think what I use is rabbit.) It comes in a granulated form that you mix with the appropriate amount of water to the strength you need, and you heat it up in a water bath to about 140 degrees Fahrenheit to melt it into a thickness you can use. I make new glue every couple of weeks, depending on what I need and what projects are in the shop.

Hide glue is great for several reasons, one of which is that it is reversible. (In all repair work, we try hard not to do anything that can't be undone if necessary.) It's also hygroscopic, so it moves and changes with humidity in a way that matches the changes in the wood, unlike most other glues which can't do this.

You can use a bit of white glue on peg collars if they come loose. You can also use a bit of white glue to tack down the edge of a thumb grip on your bow if that's coming loose. I use a bit of white glue to attach the nut to the end of the fingerboard, but you should never be in a position to have to do that. Those are the spots where you don't need hide glue. Everything else? You need hide glue.

Doesn't matter what kind of woodworking the super-handy-family-member does who holds up a bottle and says they can save you a trip to your luthier. Any other glue is simply going to cause problems later, particularly any kind of carpenter's glue, or Titebond, or anything with a gorilla on it. You are not actually saving time or money if undoing the wrong thing will end up costing more of both than simply having it done right to start with.

Just go to your luthier. We're nice, we like to see you, and we have the right glue.

CHAPTER 4

VARNISH

Violin varnish is gravely misunderstood by nearly everybody. And this guide isn't really the place to go into all of that, but there are basic things players should know.

There are two basic reasons for adding varnish to a violin: The first is protection, the second is beauty. Without varnish, violins are too vulnerable to the elements and basic wear and tear to last long. Varnish also greatly enhances the beauty of the wood, and luthiers are specialized woodworkers who want to create lovely things. Varnish is important for making violins last, and making them look like something we're glad will last.

Varnish is generally considered a sacred part of the instrument, so no luthier worth anything would ever agree to strip a decent violin at the request of a customer. I've had people ask, and I always say no.

Varnish impacts the sound of your instrument, and applying it is considered half the work of building a violin.

The funny thing with varnish is that people who make it are trying to strike a balance. It should be hard enough that it protects the instrument, but not so hard that it's brittle and chips off easily. It should be soft enough to resist chipping, but not so soft that it imprints—which means it picks up texture off of things, like the inside of a case. Most commercial instruments are done with spirit varnish, which dissolves in alcohol, and is on the brittle side. Many handmade instruments are done with oil varnish, some types of which are quite durable, and some of which I've seen come off an instrument merely with water.

In general, you should not be touching the varnish on your instrument. Some people repeatedly wear off the varnish on one of the shoulders of their instrument through repeated handling, and that should be addressed before it gets too bad. Once you wear down to the ground (which is essentially the treated wood itself that lies under the varnish) you can start working dirt into the wood. A luthier can either keep putting new retouch varnish on that area, or put some other form of protection there to prevent repeated damage.

If you have an instrument that has suffered imprinting, that can usually be addressed by a luthier. Some texture problems cannot.

If you have a nice instrument, don't mess with the varnish. That means don't try to clean your strings with alcohol which could get on it, don't leave your instrument in the sun, don't let it sit in a hot car (or a cold car for that matter—uh, just don't leave it in the car, it could get stolen that way), and don't rub weird oils on it.

And there are no good commercial polishes out there in my opinion. You just end up with waxy stuff building up over time on your varnish and making everything worse later, however satisfying it is to make things look shiny in the moment. Wipe your instrument down with a dry soft cloth after every time you play to keep the rosin from collecting on it, and that's enough. If it needs a real cleaning, take it to a luthier.

But there are also instruments worth little where the integrity of the varnish is not an issue, and violins in my rental fleet that have too much varnish damage to make them presentable, I do strip and use for varnishing practice. Even in those cases, though, I can't think of any retouch tips that I think people without specific training should do. If you are having varnish issues, take it to a luthier.

People often ask me why the neck is not varnished the same way as the rest of the instrument. I've even had some people come in when they finally noticed and are alarmed that something is wrong. Varnishing the neck would be impractical because 1) It would wear off quickly from being handled all the time, and 2) It would not be as comfortable under your hands. There are several ways to finish a neck, but most people I know polish it out using shellac and a bit of mineral oil, and then several successively finer rounds of abrasive. If the neck on your instrument is starting to feel sticky or uneven or look dirty, take it to a luthier. That's not a hard fix.

DO NOT PUT ANY ADHESIVES ON VIOLIN VARNISH.

No stickers. No blue tape. No masking tape. No Scotch tape, ticker tape, a mix tape…NO TAPE. I once had a fractional violin returned to me that the teacher had covered the back of with moleskin—that soft stuff with strong adhesive backing to use on your feet. Yikes. It tore the varnish off that little violin right down to the ground coat. If you find yourself thinking about doing something similar, please stop and remember not to put adhesives on violin varnish.

I know teachers who put bits of tape on an instrument to show where to position a shoulder rest, where to guide the bow, and ironically enough to protect the edge of the C-bout. It's most often blue painters tape, and I'm sure what people do is test a bit of it on a violin, discover nothing terrible happens when they pulled it back up right away, and then assume it will be fine. But time plus adhesive equals disaster. Tape gets gummy and weird the longer it's in contact with varnish, and the varnish gets gummy and weird right back.

The best rule of thumb I can give teachers is this: "If you wouldn't do it to your own instrument, don't do it to someone else's." (And if you don't respect your own instrument enough, imagine doing whatever it is to a Strad. Then don't.)

Some varnish issues aren't that hard for a luthier to address. Varnish chipped off of edges, for instance, isn't hard to repair. Small dings, particularly on the top, aren't hard to tone down. But large scratches or scrapes become part of an instrument's story, and there often isn't too much anyone can do.

Many times varnish damage is a clue to a bad habit that a player should address. If I see similar nicks and scrapes all in a single area on a rental violin, I usually sit the parent and the player down to figure out what is happening. Many times it's related to their frog scraping against the top when they put their violin in rest position. Sometimes it's because their thumbnail is too long on their bow hand and it's digging into the top when they play pizzicato. It's seldom something the player is aware of, and it's good to diagnose and stop such habits early. There is also some varnish damage that is an indication of something wrong with the instrument itself, such as a twisted neck that angles the player's bow so that it hits a C-bout regularly. Whatever it is, don't take small scratches and chips for granted. They are information about something that needs to be corrected about how a player handles their violin.

I think the most poignant varnish issue I deal with is tears. When someone is crying while playing their instrument, tears hit the top and run at an angle across it and over the edge. If tears are not removed immediately, they leave tracks. I spent the first couple of years cleaning up rental violins in my shop wondering how people were spilling liquid on their instruments and under the tailpiece. Then I tried to correct something about my daughter's playing as she was practicing for her lesson...and a tear rolled down her cheek and onto her violin. I suddenly recognized what all those stains were. That remains my saddest professional discovery. (And those tear stains are not easy to polish out.)

So be careful with your instrument and its varnish. You are your violin's caretaker during your part of its lifetime. Try not to leave too many scars.

CHAPTER 5

TRACKING DOWN A BUZZ

This is a big category, because there are as many sources of a buzz as there are parts that can come loose on an instrument. A buzz can take seconds to find, or days, or may never be found. When people walk into my shop with a buzz, I require that they make it happen in front of me. About half the time they cannot make it buzz and it is cured without my doing anything. It's like I scared it, which is fine by me.

Often the source of that kind of intermittent buzz was a piece of clothing or jewelry. Buttons, necklaces, and zippers can all rattle against an instrument. Check for those kinds of things before doing anything else.

Tracking down a buzz is a process. Here are the questions I ask people to answer before they bring me a buzzy instrument:

- When did it start?
- What changed? (As in, did you just put on new strings? Did you drop it?)
- Is the buzz happening on open strings, fingered notes, or both?
- Is it only on certain notes?
- Are there times when it's worse?
- Would you say the buzz sounds metallic or wooden?
- Does it come and go, or is it there all the time?
- Have you tried turning it off and turning it back on again?
  (I don't actually ask that one, but I think it every time.)

All of these things help provide clues so I know where to start looking.

The current list I keep by my bench of things to check in order of likeliness and ease of repair is this:

    Seams
    Nut
    Fine Tuner
    Tailgut/Tailpiece
    Shoulder Rest
    Chinrest
    Pegs
    Fingerboard
    Strings
    Varnish in f-hole wings
    Linings
    Corners
    Glue under saddle
    Purfling
    Daleks

So let's start with my list and work from there. (And I know I won't hit everything, because there is always some new way to cause a buzz.)

SEAMS

I would say the most common cause of buzzing I encounter is open seams. The top and back plates are glued to the ribs with a weaker glue in order to give the instrument a chance to open a seam if conditions are affecting the instrument enough that it needs to relieve tension. An open seam is the sign of something going right, not wrong. It's like a tripped circuit breaker. It's helping intercept a potentially bigger problem.

The first way to check for open seams is simply to look. Often if one has popped you can see it, and even squeeze it shut if you try. Some are hard to see. The second way is to knock lightly around the outer edges of the plates to listen for a louder, more hollow sound in one spot. I have a small paint knife that I've filed down very thin that I use to carefully go around instruments to check seams.

We glue seams with hide glue. (We glue nearly everything with hide glue.)

I have special edge clamps that have clearance for the particular shape of the edges of a violin, viola, or cello. We always do the top and the back seams separately so we can position the instrument in a way that prevents glue from running down along the inside of the ribs and potentially causing new problems down the line.

All this to say that if you have an open seam, take it to a luthier. We have the proper tools to do the job, and anything else will likely cause damage and more problems later. Do not use the wrong glue in a seam. Do not let someone convince you hide glue from a bottle will be good enough. Seams are an easy fix and most shops should be able to turn that repair around by the next day, or even the same day if there is enough time for the glue to dry. There is no reason to risk your instrument's long term functioning over a simple seam.

NUT

The next most likely cause of buzzing is the nut.

The nut is usually made of ebony. In rare cases they can be made of something like bone or ivory, and too many times on cheap instruments they are something like maple that has been painted black. The softer the material used to make the nut, the more often you are likely to have problems with it.

The nut's job is to hold the strings up off that end of the fingerboard. Over time, the strings—both through the slicing motion of going back and forth through tuning, and vibrating side to side—change the string slots.

If the strings have cut through the nut to the point where the strings are now sitting on the board, they buzz.

Another common cause of buzzing at the nut is that the front of the string slot gets wider and the string can start zapping in that space. The slot needs to be adjusted at that point with a tool called a mouse-tail file.

A quick way to check the string height at the nut (and what I usually do when I'm doing a general inspection of instruments at a school) is to slide a business card under the strings toward the nut. Not under all the strings at once—just the top one alone. You should be able to reach the nut without real resistance. If the card gets stuck before you ever reach the nut, the nut needs to be raised. Sometimes people jam stuff under the string to raise the height of the string off the board that way. In a pinch, if it works, fine. But it looks goofy and is not the best option in the long term.

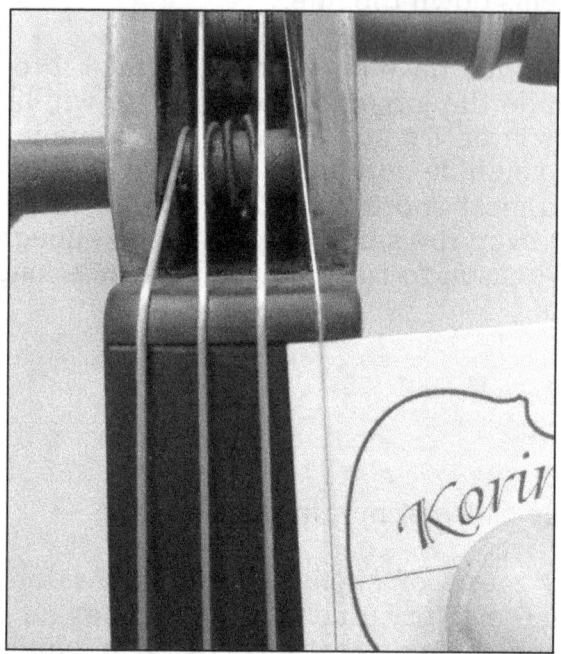

If you are having buzzing on just open strings, then it's most likely the nut. Take it to a luthier.

FINE TUNERS

Ah, fine tuners. They are like a well of buzzing that never runs dry. If you need fine tuners on all of your strings, use a tailpiece that has them all built into it. There are several reasons for this, including not choking off the after-length, not causing damage to the top, but most relevant to this chapter because tuners you add to a tailpiece have extra parts. Those little parts all come loose and rattle at some point.

If you have at least one added-on fine tuner, check to see if the little nut holding it in place needs tightening. I just do that with needle-nose pliers, but you can over tighten and hurt the tailpiece if you're not careful, so it's a completely reasonable thing to have a luthier do for you if you want, even though it's easy. But if you want to do that on your own, just be gentle.

Putting wax on the threading of fine tuner screws is often helpful. Not only will it make the tuner move more smoothly, but it can prevent the screw from rattling in the nut. I use beeswax or paraffin.

TAILGUT / TAILPIECE

Most tailguts are plastic and held in with a pair of nuts you screw into place. Sometimes there are extra little pieces to go with them that rattle, or sometimes the end of the tailgut is too long and buzzes against the top of the instrument. In a few cases I've seen violas where the tailgut was buzzing inside the holes coming out of the tail—something probably to do with the laxer tension on violas compared to violins—and the buzz was solved by jamming a toothpick in there. I mention this because I find it interesting, but I don't really want people jamming toothpicks into their instruments. Just take it to a luthier.

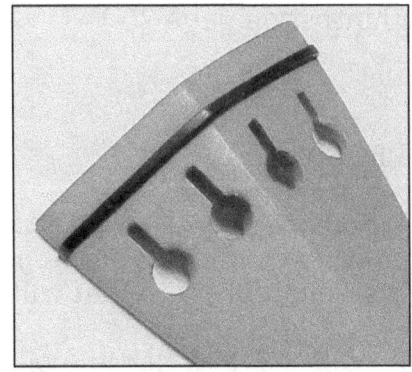

On a tailpiece where the tuners are not built in, there is an extra little lip that holds the strings up off the tailpiece itself that is referred to as a saddle. (Yes, I know I already called the ebony piece that the tailgut runs over the "saddle," but that's one of those words we use too many places, like "button.")

If that piece comes unglued it can cause buzzing. If you know for sure that the tailpiece saddle is loose, and you think you can safely get a bit of white glue in there to secure it, go ahead. You'll need to either secure it with a small clamp (clothespins wrapped with rubber bands to make them grippy often works), or hold it with your fingers for at least ten minutes. (I find a good movie to watch when I need to be a human clamp.) White glue takes about twenty minutes to dry. If gluing the saddle on a tailpiece back in place makes you uncomfortable, take it to a luthier.

SHOULDER REST

The first thing I usually do when someone has made an instrument buzz for me, is I take off their shoulder rest and see if the buzz goes away or not. People often overlook that as a source of something vibrating, but if the adjustment screws are loose, they can rattle. I've also seen instances where the shoulder rest was tilting to the point where the middle of it was in contact with the back of the instrument and that caused a buzz.

CHINREST

The second thing I usually do is remove the chinrest. If the chinrest is touching the tailpiece it can buzz. Keep in mind that in some cases the chinrest only touches the tailpiece while you are pressing your chin down on it. (Which is another reason it's important to me that the player make the instrument buzz, and not expect me to reproduce the problem. I may not hold the instrument in a way that mimics how the player is using it and miss something.)

The chinrest can buzz if it's too loose, or has a crack in it. If it's obviously too loose, tighten it. If it has a crack, replace it. (Review how to tighten a chinrest on page 25.)

PEGS

When ornaments on pegs come loose, they buzz. If the collar is a different color from the rest of the peg (such as an ebony ring on a boxwood peg) it is a separate piece that will likely come loose at some point, and will buzz.

If you have a loose collar and you are feeling wild, you have my permission to tack that down with a little white glue. (Just don't get glue on anything else, please. Or, you know, you could take it to a luthier.)

Same with the little decorative ball/pip on the end. Those come loose all the time and cause buzzing. You can check if that's the problem by holding the pip securely with your fingers as you play and see if the buzz disappears. This can be fixed with a little white glue.

If you hear buzzing from a peg that has pips, but don't see anything moving, and holding the pip still doesn't help, there could be a little piece of something like old glue vibrating away just underneath it inside the peg head. If you want to preserve those pips, take it to a luthier. (I know many people who find those pips more trouble than they are worth, and simply remove them all as a preemptive strike against buzzing.)

FINGERBOARD

For student instruments, first check the finger tapes. Sometimes the nut might not be technically too low for the instrument to function, but the added thickness of tapes messes with that. (Fingerboards are not varnished, so tape is safe to use. I recommend detailing tape from the automotive supply store, by the way. It's very thin and not as awful to clean up later.)

People can see that fingerboards are curved the short direction, but most people don't realize that the length of the board is concave. The strings spin like a jump rope—wider in the middle—and there needs to be clearance or else the string zaps against the board. Sometimes there is not enough scoop in the board and some strings or notes buzz. Sometimes there are lumps in the board and only certain fingerings buzz. Over time fingerboards wear down and the strings can create grooves, and pits can develop where the fingers press repeatedly. Periodically fingerboards need to be re-planed to even out that surface again. This is called a "fingerboard dressing," and the frequency of it varies depending on the player and the instrument.

Buzzes that only happen on specific notes (often ones new to the player being learned in a higher position) are frequently caused by flaws in the fingerboard. Take it to a luthier.

STRINGS

Sometimes strings are bad right out of the box. If you put on new strings and one of them is instantly weird, put the old one back on and see if the problem goes away. If it does, get a new string.

Sometimes the act of changing strings can unsettle something somewhere on an instrument. Those are usually cases where it disappears by the time someone brings it to me, and I get credit for scaring the buzz away.

Another thing to check for is misbehaving string protectors. E-strings in particular always come with a plastic "noodle" that you can lay in the string slot of the bridge, and if that has gotten caught in the pegbox, or in the after-length, or is just not resting correctly on the bridge, it can buzz. If you have protection on the bridge already in the form of a parchment or drum skin, that noodle protector is not needed. I always remove the noodle to eliminate that potential for buzzing.

VARNISH IN THE F-HOLE WINGS

This was my biggest buzz nightmare story in the early days of my shop. A guy brought in a violin with a horrible nasty buzz that had just started out of nowhere and would not go away. Sounded like a cicada was stuck in the instrument. I worked on it for three days. I opened and re-glued seams. I changed the strings, I changed the tailpiece, I changed the chinrest, I checked the nut....

I did everything I could think of, then started calling all the other luthiers I knew for advice. My teacher was the one who finally asked, "Did you check the varnish in the f-holes?" And that was it. A ten second fix with a bridge knife to clear out some varnish that had been stuck at the bottom of a lower wing. After years of playing, that little bit of varnish had finally cracked loose and was buzzing like crazy.

So this cause of buzzing is rare, but I always check for it early, because it has come across my path a few times since. (And I think it goes without saying that you should not be going at your instrument with a knife, so if you know this is the problem, take it to a luthier.)

LININGS

Or the bass bar. Or something goofy with the blocks. Or even the label.

There are internal things that can come loose and cause buzzing. (But not the soundpost. People often tell me they are worried about their soundpost buzzing, but I personally have never seen that happen.) When linings come loose, you can usually figure that out by pressing on the plates like you are squeezing a seam shut, and the buzzing will stop as the instrument is played. The fix is usually a matter of opening up the rib in the area and re-gluing it, and that's enough to get glue to the lining.

If it's something internal that requires removing the top of your instrument to get to, I'm really sorry. (Thankfully that's uncommon.)

CORNERS

If it's something goofy in your corners it's unlikely you'll figure that out. It will be hard for your luthier to figure it out, so be patient.

GLUE UNDER THE SADDLE

Yeah, that's a hard one to find. Any spot a little piece of glue can break off and get trapped can be a nightmare to locate. I know someone who once found glue rattling around under a fingerboard. The worst story I know was about a bit of glue under a patch, *under another patch,* inside a top that I think was removed and inspected at least twice before the luthier found it.

PURFLING

Same thing. Purfling is an inlay, which means it's set into a channel with glue, and if some little part of that comes loose and starts buzzing essentially inside your plate.... Ugh. Luckily, I've never had to deal with this, but I know people who have, so I always keep it in mind as a possibility.

DALEKS

Or any aliens. Or ghosts. Or who knows? When I'm baffled, sometimes I take out my sonic screwdriver and pass it over the instrument with a blue light and a wobbly-whirring sound that some people actually think is doing something. (But any Dr. Who fan would know that the real joke is that sonic screwdrivers don't work on wood.) Sometimes it feels impossible to locate a buzz, and when we keep eliminating possibilities but it persists, the issue starts to feel supernatural. (At this stage there can be swearing involved.)

One other thing that is not on my list but should be mentioned: Bridges. Bridges don't generally buzz. I'm saying generally because I have never seen a bridge be the cause of a buzz, although a close colleague said she saw it once when the parchment came loose, and that sounds completely reasonable, but it still hasn't happened in front of me. However, people come to me all the time convinced the bridge is causing a buzz, and that has never once been the case. Doesn't mean it can't happen, but when trying to diagnose the cause of a buzz, probably don't start there.

Anyway, the first part of this list is useful to actual players and teachers, and the rest of it is just to illustrate how varied and complicated it can get. If I can fix a buzz in under ten minutes, I often don't charge for it. Sometimes I spend hours with an instrument and have to charge something for my time even if I can't solve it.

All this to say that "a buzz" is not some universal problem with an instant solution. Take it to your luthier. But have pity on them.

One last thing: A Wolf Note is not a buzz. It's a whole different problem. They don't come up often on violin. (There is one nasty wolf way high up on the G string that violinists find when working on a particular concerto —Saint Saens possibly—that requires they sit on a C or C#, and then they stumble on the wolf and freak out.) I almost never come across a wolf on a viola, but they can be anywhere. It is a common problem on cello, so if you are curious about wolves, skip ahead to Chapter 9, "Notes About Cellos."

CHAPTER 6

WHAT TO KNOW ABOUT YOUR BOW

BASIC BOW MAINTENANCE

The most important thing to remember about your bow, is always remove tension from it when it's not in use. Particularly when it's traveling in your case. A bow under tension is a zillion times more likely to break than one that isn't. (I'm pretty sure that's the statistic.)

Next, don't touch the hair. Rosin plus the oil on your fingers equals some kind of dirt magnet that will shorten the life of the horsehair.

Never never never ever tap the tip of your bow against anything if you can help it. This includes tapping your bow against your stand as a means of applause no matter how well someone played. (Shuffle or stomp your feet instead. It's old school, and safer for both your instrument and bow.)

Get a rehair about once a year. During a rehair, a luthier can clean your bow, and examine all of it and point out any problems.

A few hairs falling out once in a while is normal. If there is a strand of loose hair you need to cut off, isolate it, and use a nail clipper to trim it at the tip or frog. If a lot of hair is falling out, that is not normal. Take it to a luthier.

I don't mind teachers putting tape on their students' bows in order to help them learn. I do mind when teachers use something sticky like a corn pad for thumb placement and overlap that adhesive onto the hair itself. That just prematurely ruins a lot of hair.

People ask me about cleaning the hair. This is not a thing. Once the hair has rosin on it, you shouldn't be messing with it. And if your bow hair is dirty enough (usually down by the frog, but I've seen bows that were dirty all over) that you notice it's dirty, the dirt isn't actually the problem. The dirt is a symptom of how much you play, and that the hair is probably stripped, and no amount of "cleaning" will fix that. You need new hair.

Wash your hands. Handling your equipment with dirty hands is never good.

MECHANICS OF A BOW

Many people don't realize when they are tightening and loosening their bows, that what they are actually doing is sliding the frog back and forth along the stick.

The length available in the stick mortise is the total range available to adjust the length of the hair. When you tighten the screw, since the button is butted up against the end of the stick and can't go anywhere, the eyelet attached to the frog moves instead.

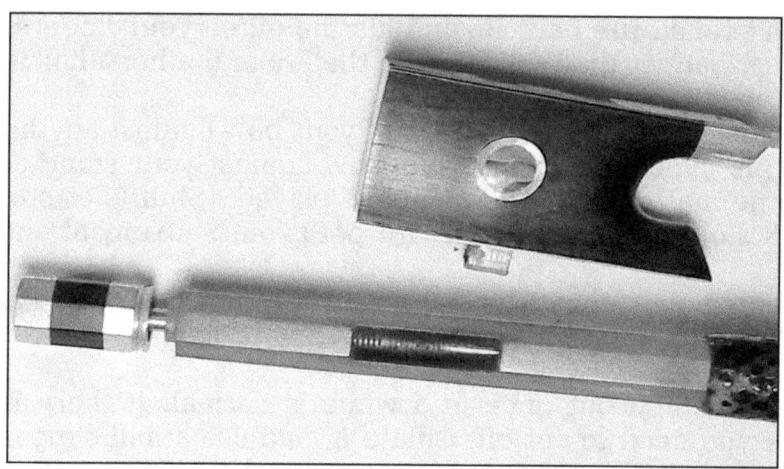

At its loosest, the frog should be at the front of the stick mortise, and right up against the thumb grip. The tighter you turn the screw, the farther the frog backs away from the thumb grip. The limit it can back up is the length of the stick mortise.

Weather is a huge factor when rehairing a bow, because hair length is impacted by humidity. Bow hair is longer when the humidity is high, and shrinks up when it is low. I try to avoid doing rehairs during heavy rainstorms, or severe cold snaps, because calculating a length to cut the hair that will work the rest of the year gets complicated.

This means the distance between the frog and thumb grip will change depending upon the weather when your bow is at the tension you like, so try not to get too attached to the specific distance of that space if you live in a dynamic climate. It may not be something your luthier can do much about unless you want to rehair your bow for each season.

If you're curious about any of this, it's perfectly safe to unscrew your button completely and take the frog off the stick to look at it. Just make sure when you put it back together that the hair isn't twisted.

It's also fine to lubricate the screw with a little paraffin to help it turn more smoothly.

REHAIRING

Rehairing is the term for replacing the hair on a bow. (Sometimes people tell me they need a "restringing" which makes me think they want me to replace the strings on their instrument, but most of the time the word they are looking for is "rehair.")

Professionals often need to change the hair on their bow more frequently than once a year, and some fiddle players in particular can literally tear through hair in a matter of days, but for the average player an annual rehair is sufficient. Don't let it go more than two. (Most of my customers tend to get new strings and hair at the same time as part of their instrument's annual checkup.)

Be aware that the average player can't tell exactly when they need a rehair. Your bow doesn't feel that different from one day to the next, so the degradation is gradual. If you jumped back several months and could feel the difference in your bow, then you would recognize how much it's changed. This is why putting that bit of maintenance on a schedule is helpful.

The biggest problem I struggle with when rehairing cheap bows, is they are not usually assembled with the idea in mind that anyone will bother rehairing them in the future, so things may be glued together that shouldn't be, and internal parts are usually not shaped correctly. Getting the slide out in particular can be quite a struggle, and I usually have to recut the frog mortise into a shape I can work with. It's a lot more work than it should be. It often makes more sense to simply replace a really cheap bow than try to rehair it.

I think the main thing I wish the average player knew about bows is that rehairing them is more art than science. It's not some mindless act of popping out an old part and putting in a new one. There is a remarkable variety of ways for bows to behave, and some are easy to work with, and some are torture.

It's important to understand rehairs are done by hand. I once received a call from a man who wanted me to rehair a hundred school bows in a weekend, and I told him that wasn't possible. He became irritated and asked me how hard was it to simply "stick them in the rehair machine." I had to explain that I was the rehair machine, and sticking them in me anywhere wasn't going to get them done any faster.

It also helps to know that part of the process of rehairing a bow is to wet the new hair before putting it on, and that needs time to dry. You can hit it with a hairdryer if there is a need to finish it quickly, but letting it dry naturally is best. I find I get the best read on whether I got the length right (and if I need to redo it) if I wait until the next day, so unless it's an emergency, I like to keep rehairs overnight.

Often people ask if I can do a rehair while they wait. The answer is no.

Did I mention you should get a rehair about once a year? Yes? Good. If you are on a basic schedule like that you don't need to worry about it. But if you're someone who wants me to tell you how to tell if you need a rehair, the first answer is: If you can't remember when you last had one, you are overdue. If it's dirty, you are overdue. If you are using a ton of rosin (more than a bit for every four hours of play or so) the hair is stripped and can't hold onto the rosin, then you are overdue. Take it to a luthier and get a rehair.

From time to time, I see players speculating about rehairing their own bows. If the goal is to save money, that's not the way to go. (It's a little like deciding to make your own elaborate wedding cake if you've never baked before, and don't own any piping bags or cake pans. The time, materials, and skill you need to obtain first don't make that a practical plan when hiring a professional is more efficient and affordable. Plus, unlike a messed up cake which might still be edible, you could accidentally damage your bow and regret it.)

If, however, rehairing bows is simply a process that interests you for its own sake, or you want to expand your skill set, that's great. Take a course where someone can supervise you and give you feedback in real time. You'll need to invest in specialized equipment and tools. Several of my tools I had to make or adjust myself. It takes many, many rehairs to get good at it, so be patient.

For what is essentially a stick with hair attached to it, a lot can go wrong. Here are a few things to be aware of:

MISSING SPREAD WEDGE

If the hair is all bunched up at the frog end, that means you lost your spread wedge somewhere. Take it to a luthier. In many cases I can cut somebody a new spread wedge. But often when that happens it turns out the bow is due for a rehair anyway, and it makes more sense to just do that.

HAIR FALLING OUT AT THE TIP

If the hair falls out at the tip, but the mortise still has a plug in it, then the knot failed. Take it to a luthier for a rehair.

If the hair falls out at the tip, and the plug is gone, take it to a luthier. If you have the old plug and it's okay (maybe just knocked out if the bow was dropped or bumped into something), bring it, and maybe it can be put back in. If the plug is bad or missing, often I can just cut a new one while the customer waits. But bows that have already been rosined are not usually too keen on being taken apart in any way and put back together again. Most of the time I'm able to cut a new plug and the bow is fine, but sometimes I have to simply rehair it.

BOW WON'T TIGHTEN

If your bow won't tighten enough, DON'T KEEP CRANKING ON THE SCREW. Sometimes people feel as if they are getting somewhere by continuing to tighten the bow past the point where it wants to stop. All that's happening is that you are pulling the button off the screw. Some people come to me with the button in hand once it's fallen off completely.

If your bow won't tighten there are a few possibilities:

The most common is you just need a rehair. Hair length is impacted by humidity. Here, the hair is longer in the summer and shorter in the winter. Ideally, I would ask people to rehair their bows twice a year if I could, once for each big shift in the seasons. But that is expensive and inconvenient for most people, so I have to do my best to find a length that can accommodate the large swings in Wisconsin weather. It doesn't always work on some bows if they have a really short mortise, so if you got a rehair when it was cold and dry out, and then you are trying to use it when it's rainy and hot, it may not be up to it. Sometimes if a person is not ready for a whole new rehair, I can go back into the bow and shorten the hair a little, and if we're lucky it all goes back together nicely. If not, it needs a rehair.

Another common possibility is that the plug inside the frog can fail, which can cause the knot to shift too far forward, changing the overall length of the hair on the bow, making it too long to tighten. It may or may not be possible to simply cut a new plug for it, and keep the existing hair. The bow might not want to go back together nicely if you simply replace the plug, in which case you'd need a rehair.

The knot inside the frog can also fail, and that usually starts off looking like the bow won't tighten, and turns into the hair just coming out at that end. Then you need a rehair.

It's also possible for the bow to not tighten because the eyelet is stripped. When this happens, people often come to me saying the screw is stripped, but it's actually the piece the screw fits into that is made of brass that may eventually fail. Take it to a luthier.

BOW WON'T LOOSEN

The other end of the spectrum is when the bow won't loosen. That's everything I just told you flipped on its head, where maybe you got a rehair during a summer rainstorm and by the time winter hits, it all shrinks up and there is no room left to loosen anything. In this case it kind of depends on the bow when deciding what to do.

I've had times here where for one week it's 40 below zero* and a bow I've rehaired becomes too tight, but the player is willing to simply undo the screw and take the frog off the stick when they aren't playing during that time, and once we get past that week, the bow is fine again. Other people want me to redo it.

The quality of the bow in question matters. A wood bow that won't loosen is at risk. The carbon fiber bows in my rental program are not. (For those, I tell customers not to worry about loosening the bow if the hair is too short. They just need to remind kids about that habit each time they put their bow away. If it really bothers them I offer to replace the bow, but I have yet to have anyone care.)

There is no way to add length to an existing rehair, so going back into the bow to adjust it is not an option the way it is when the hair is too long.

[*Weird piece of temperature trivia: 40 below is the only temperature that is the same in Fahrenheit as in Celsius, so this example works however you read it!]

WRAP IS COMING LOOSE

I described the different kinds of wraps in the earlier vocabulary chapter, and different types may need to be dealt with differently. If your wrap is a little loose, a luthier can usually tack it down. If you're having an issue with the whole thing starting to unravel and you want to secure it temporarily with some kind of tape until you can get it to a luthier, that's okay. If just the end of the wrap is coming loose or starting to unravel, that can usually be solved by adding a collar.

Be aware that if the wrap needs to be replaced, the thumb grip has to be removed to do that, so you will also be paying for a new thumb grip (if that isn't already factored into the price quote).

THUMB GRIP IS COMING LOOSE

The thumb grip is held in place with basic white glue. If a little edge of the grip starts to come up, you can go ahead and put a little dot of white glue under it and hold it in place for several minutes. Give it about 20 minutes to fully dry before you use the bow again. That's all the magic I use for that.

If the thumb grip is worn through or sliding all over the place, take it to a luthier.

FERRULE HAS COME LOOSE

If the ferrule comes off the frog and is sliding loose on the hair, it means you've also lost your spread wedge, and you should take it to a luthier.

HEADPLATE IS BROKEN

If the headplate is broken, it depends on the bow and exactly how broken you're talking.

The headplate's job is to absorb some of the impact the tip of the bow typically suffers in order to protect the wood. It's not uncommon at all to replace a headplate, so if it gets damaged, you should have someone put on a new one. Even small cracks can make a good bow too vulnerable for many people to want to rehair it before you get that addressed.

However, on an inexpensive bow where the cost of a new headplate rivals the worth of the whole stick, I've seen people choose to live with a certain amount of damage and take the risk, and I've gone ahead and rehaired their bow anyway.

If you want to replace a headplate, you will also have to get a rehair. So don't pay for a rehair and then decide a week later you do actually want a new headplate—plan for the two things together.

Take notice of your headplate. Many players are startled when they bring their bows to me for a rehair and I point out that their nose, or even their entire headplate is gone.

MY BOW DOESN'T HAVE ENOUGH RESISTANCE ANYMORE

The camber has probably gone out of it. Take it to a luthier. (Or maybe invest in a new bow, depending on the situation.)

MY BOW IS WARPED

Take it to a luthier, and see if they can either adjust it with a rehair, or straighten it. (Or, again, maybe invest in a new bow, depending on the situation.)

THE STICK HAS SNAPPED / HEAD HAS BROKEN

If the bow is expensive or historic, I hope you have insurance. In many cases the bow can be repaired back to decent playing condition, but it's not cheap, and the appraisal value of the bow is completely compromised.

If it's a student stick? It's done. You can use it as a tomato stake.

The bow is half your instrument. It's your voice when you play. A bad one can hold you back and make playing frustrating beyond belief. If you've never considered investing in a decent bow, it's a good thing to explore.

Bows can be delicate tools. Treat them nicely. Don't touch the hair.

And again, don't tap your bow on a stand as a means of applause. I have a (bow) tip jar on my counter as a result of such moments.

CHAPTER 7

NOTES ABOUT CELLOS

I have spent this book primarily referring to violins and violas, since that is where my greater knowledge lies, and most of this information applies to cellos as well. However, there is information specific to cellos that I'll address briefly here.

(Side note: The plural of "cello" can be "cellos" or "celli." Webster's lists "cellos" first, and it sounds less affected to me, so that's what I use. I mean, technically, we should be putting an apostrophe before the "c" either way, because "cello" is short for "violoncello," which is the formal name for the instrument. "Violon" means bass violin, and since in this case we're talking about a smaller version of an actual bass, the "cello" part added on is to indicate it's "small," so we're describing a "small big violin." Weird how we've shortened the name so that the largest instrument in a traditional string quartet is called the "small." Regardless of all of that....)

Cellos are big, which makes them more vulnerable to all kinds of injuries. There is a lot more surface area on them to move and change and encounter disaster out in the world. Cellos get left on the floor unattended more often than violins or violas do. Never step over a cello. Never let anyone else step over a cello. I've seen too many cellos that have been tripped over or had a foot go through them.

We used to rent cellos at my store, but they were all coming back smashed and it was too depressing. (Not to mention expensive.) A hard case is a good idea to have for something as large and fragile as a cello, but in all honesty, there were very few instances where the case would have saved one of the cellos in my rental program.

Even though hard cases are a good idea, the vast majority of injuries that happen to cellos tend to occur during circumstances that deviated from the player's daily routine when the instrument was already out of the case, like at a concert or a dress rehearsal on an unfamiliar stage. People behave differently in new surroundings, and the potential for mishaps increases, especially for cellos.

CELLO BRIDGES

There are two basic types of bridges for cello: French and Belgian.

French Bridge Blank   Belgian Bridge Blank

For student cellos in particular, the French tends to be the better option because there is more room for a variety of heights, and cutting things down too low on a Belgian bridge gets weird.

Regardless of the type of bridge, the important thing to know for cello is that many people need one for winter and one for summer (depending on their instrument and where they live). When the humidity is high, so are the string heights. When the humidity is low, the string heights go down. This has to do again with the vast amount of surface area you're dealing with on a cello, and how the body of the instrument is reacting to the weather. So a bridge that may feel fine in the summer may be too low when winter rolls around, and even cause the strings to buzz against the fingerboard. Or a bridge that is fine in the winter may be unbearably tall come summer. I have several customers who come in every six months to have me switch out their bridge.

An interesting note about cellos and their after-length: It's long enough on cellos they should be tuned. I was taught the length of the tailgut is correct when the after-length on the C-string plays a G when you pluck it.

The descriptions earlier about checking to make sure if the bridge is standing straight apply to cellos, but with some added considerations because of their size. To nudge a violin or a viola bridge into standing up straight, I don't loosen the strings at all. I do when I adjust the straightness of a cello bridge. I don't do it much, but a cello bridge is definitely harder to move when it's under full tension, so loosen the strings a little. A cello is also too cumbersome to hold easily in your lap, so find a soft, stable surface to rest it on. (I have a dedicated surface for working on cellos called a "cradle," but in the average home a couch or a bed will do.) All the other rules about placing your thumbs together in the middle of the top of the bridge, and sighting it from the bass-side, apply.

ROMBERGS

Another thing specific to cellos is a fingerboard with a Romberg. Violin fingerboards are an even curve the whole width. Cellos can be that way, or they can have an angled flat surface just under the C string, and that flat surface is called a Romberg. (Some violas have a tiny Romberg, and given the option I always reshape the board and take them out. They are somebody's weird aspiration to make violas more cello-like in my opinion, but it's unnecessary, and in certain instances a hindrance. Violists don't need to be cellists. We are plenty great as we are.)

You can like or not like the Romberg as you please, but be aware that if the nut isn't lined up with it correctly, or it doesn't work with the bridge placement, it can cause issues, such as the G string winding up right on that ridge rather than comfortably to the side of it. If you think the

Romberg is contributing to some sort of fingering problem, take it to a luthier.

ENDPINS

There are different types of endpins for cello, and cellists have all kinds of opinions on them. If the whole endpin as it fits into the cello is loose or angled badly, take it to a luthier.

If the rod itself is sticking as you take it in and out of the endpin, you can try lubricating it with graphite. (Or take it to a luthier who will probably lubricate it with graphite.)

If the point of the endpin rod gets dull, a luthier can sharpen it again, although I suppose I wouldn't object if someone had a decent mill file and wanted to do it themselves. (But only if you can remove the entire rod and do that work away from the cello.)

WOLF NOTES

Wolf notes are not a problem exclusive to cellos, but more prevalent with them.

A wolf is a spot on a string that when you hold it still, the pitch starts to wobble almost like you are doing vibrato even though you are not. It's weird and hard to control.

All cellos have a wolf. I've even met players who love theirs, but most people want it gone. If you're lucky, yours is hidden between two notes so you don't land on it very often, if ever. If you are less lucky, it's right on something useful like an F# that you need all the time.

There are several ways to go after a wolf, and what works on one cello may not work the same way on another. This is something you need to have patience with while a luthier tries several things. I don't recommend you just buy a random wolf eliminator, or even one recommended by another player that happened to work on their cello, and start messing with it yourself. It saves time (and possibly a string) by having someone with experience work with you to shift the wolf someplace unobtrusive.

SEAMS

Cellos have more issues with seams than violins and violas do, simply because there is so much more length of them to deal with, and so much more surface area in general that is affected by weather. Cellists with older instruments would be wise to budget to have seams glued every fall.

CELLO BOWS

Cello bows are shorter, thicker, and heavier than their violin and viola counterparts. Rehairs for cello bows typically cost a little more because they require more hair.

(Cellos are great. Sorry if you felt neglected up to this point in this book!)

CHAPTER 8

QUICK TIPS FOR TEACHERS IN SCHOOLS

First of all, let me explain that for much of the advice in this book when I say "teacher," I am primarily thinking of private teachers, who are generally not burdened with budgeting for maintenance and repairs for their students' equipment.

I am advocating best practices, and habits that apply to the best instruments. Even if we are not in a position to follow through, it's still important to understand the ideal, and aspire to it. It helps to know where the standards are.

That said, most teachers in school settings are in rather desperate circumstances repair-wise. I am not insensitive to that.

I work with a lot of schools and see a lot of frustrating things. Teachers who struggle in school settings without a decent budget don't have the luxury of proper maintenance work. Many are even tossed into circumstances where they have to manage string programs, and they know relatively little about strings at all.

This chapter aims to be a reference for more of the day-to-day issues those teacher face in schools where every day can feel like an emergency.

TRACKING YOUR INSTRUMENTS

Every instrument in your fleet should have an identifying number, preferably directly on the instrument, not just its case. If you have a means of placing a sticker inside through the bass side f-hole, that's ideal, but not feasible for many. If marking the outside of the instrument, I recommend doing it on the rib down by the endbutton. Some schools do this with small aluminum tags bent to the curve of the rib and secured in place with rubber cement. Others use a paint pen. I know several that engrave the number into the wood, but personally I'm opposed to this unless you have impeccable handwriting.

Keep a spreadsheet of what each instrument is in terms of type of instrument and size, inventory number, serial number if it has one, and which student has been entrusted with it.

When I do work for schools, I keep a record of all the repairs both completed, or needed, for each instrument, and share that with the teacher if they want. If you don't have a luthier, it's not a bad idea for you to track such things yourself. That makes it easier to budget for what you need when funds are available.

TUNING ISSUES

This is the most common problem I encounter with school instruments, and few things are more maddening than trying to teach someone on an instrument that can't be tuned.

This is important enough you should go and carefully read the detailed descriptions in Chapter 2, if you haven't already, for how to change strings, what to do if pegs are slipping, and what to do if they are sticking.

But to summarize the most basic points: If a peg is slipping, check the way the strings are wound, and if the string hole needs to be re-drilled. These two things fix the vast majority of tuning problems in my experience with school instruments.

The other possibility when pegs aren't working is Caspari pegs, which unfortunately I see in a lot of old school instruments. They are thick, and have screws on the ends. If those are slipping, you are supposed to be able to tighten them with a special screwdriver, but it is next to impossible you have one thin enough to work. This is by design—I don't have one either. And if the whole shaft of the peg has come loose, there may not be an affordable way to deal with it on a school budget. (Those pegs are the worst.)

SCHOOL TEACHERS NEED PEG DOPE

Inexpensive instruments are cheap for several reasons, not the least of which is they rarely have been set up properly. (That amount of labor adds to their cost.) During initial set up, peg holes should be treated with peg dope, but this step is usually skipped on cheap violins, so school teachers are then tasked with doing that themselves. Keep a stick of peg dope in your tool kit (I use Hill) and use it liberally on any pegs that stick.

FINE TUNERS

When possible, try to switch out small tailpieces that have to have tuners added to every string, to something like a Wittner tailpiece that has the tuners built in. They are better all around. (Easier to use, less frequent buzzing issues, less damaging to strings and the top of the instrument, better sound.)

If you are struggling with those miserable little fine tuners that you have to thread the strings under, you have my sympathy. They are awful. I don't know how to help you with those.

WHEN A BRIDGE FALLS DOWN

This is the number one problem teachers ask me about when I do professional development workshops in public schools. Unfortunately, many of those instruments have poorly made bridges, so I understand why the question comes up so often. I don't advise a teacher to try and stand up a bridge on a better instrument, but they should know what to do with the average school violin.

First, check that the post is still standing inside. If not, you can't put the bridge back up until that's fixed. (Set that aside for a luthier to do.) If the post is fine, loosen the strings just enough that you can slip the bridge back into place without having to force the feet to scrape against the top.

Make sure the bridge is facing the right direction! The BACK of the bridge should be FLAT. The TREBLE side of the bridge is LOWER and usually has some sort of protector on the highest slot.

Place the bridge between the inner f-hole notches. If there were a line connecting those notches, the bridge feet would have that line running right through the middle of them.

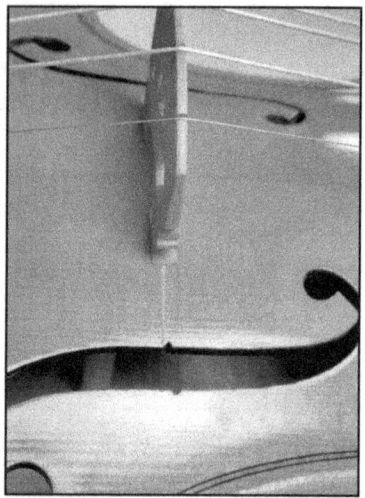

You want the bridge centered, and parallel between the fingerboard and the tailpiece—not at an angle at all. You then need to check the side to side placement of the bridge by making sure the strings look even on the fingerboard from the front view. It can also helps to sight the board from the nut end, and see if the bridge looks even from that view, too.

Tune up, check the bridge to make sure it's not leaning (the back of the bridge should look perpendicular to the top of the instrument), and go. (Read about checking bridge straightness in Chapter 2.)

If a bridge repeatedly falls down, it's either not fitted right at the feet, or it's warped. A luthier needs to check the feet. For a warped bridge if a luthier is not an option, find a tutorial you're comfortable with to straighten it yourself. (I just heard every luthier reading this book gasp. Jump ahead to the end of Chapter 9 to see why I am not so worried. And remember, this may be the difference between a kid having a violin, or no violin. Personally, I'd rather they have a violin.)

CLEANING INSTRUMENTS

I am very nervous about giving advice about this, but I know school teachers need to do something about when their students' instruments get filthy. I know there are things that work on cheap instruments that would be horrible on a good ones. I want to encourage practices that can be used on either, so good things don't get ruined by mistake.

I am going to advise against any sort of polish. It probably won't harm a cheap student violin, but it's not a good habit to apply commercial polish.

For basic smudges and fingerprints, just use a dry cloth, and don't be afraid to rub hard. The only places where pressure while using a cloth can be dangerous is around the f-hole wings where you can cause cracks if you push down too hard. In those areas, concentrate on moving across the surface more than down.

For some grime, you can use a paper towel with a bit of water, but whatever water you get on, rub right off. Water left on varnish can leave spots. (And on some instruments, you can strip the varnish right off with water, so be careful. But most little instruments with industrial-strength-student-violin-varnish should be fine.)

If you have lots of gross dirty rosin stuck to an instrument, you can try a couple of different de-greasers, like Simple Green or Citrisolv. Apply a VERY SMALL AMOUNT to a bit of paper towel—DON'T put the solvents directly on the instrument—and rub at the grime. After cleaning with those products, I'd go over it again with water, and then again with a dry cloth.

Be aware that when luthiers clean an unfamiliar instrument, we always test what we're doing under the chinrest where any mishaps with the varnish are less noticeable. Cleaning can be tricky. Never be cavalier about it. But on typical little warhorse violins you should be safe.

RETOUCHING DINGS

Don't. I'm in total favor of making all instruments presentable, but retouch you should really leave to professionals. (I do it for free on most school instruments. See if your local luthier is up for that kind of volunteer work—you never know.)

If your school has room in its budget to address varnish issues, do it. It's worth the investment to make instruments look good because they are less likely to be abused. Instruments I've stripped and re-varnished for schools have fewer problems afterwards, because when they look worthy of respect, students treat them that way.

CLEANING STRINGS

I hate recommending anything here, either, but again in schools it can be sort of an emergency, and there are different rules.

If you are careful not to get anything on the varnish, you can use basic alcohol wipes to get crud off strings. You can also use 0000 steel wool. (Or 3200 grit micromesh if you can find it, but most people don't have access to that.)

Do this sparingly. The more you clean your strings, the more you degrade them, which goes against the entire purpose of continuing to use them long after they should have been changed.

IDENTIFYING THINGS IN YOUR INVENTORY

When asking teachers in schools what kinds of things they hoped to find in this book, the basics of simply telling certain things apart kept coming up. Many teachers inherit a stockpile of instruments and bows in a classroom and have to sort out for themselves what they've even got. Teachers whose expertise is in wind or brass instruments often find strings confusing. I hope these next few entries will help. And if you have further questions, contact a luthier.

TELLING SMALL VIOLINS AND SMALL VIOLAS APART

Basically, violas have taller ribs, so they look thicker/taller from the side.

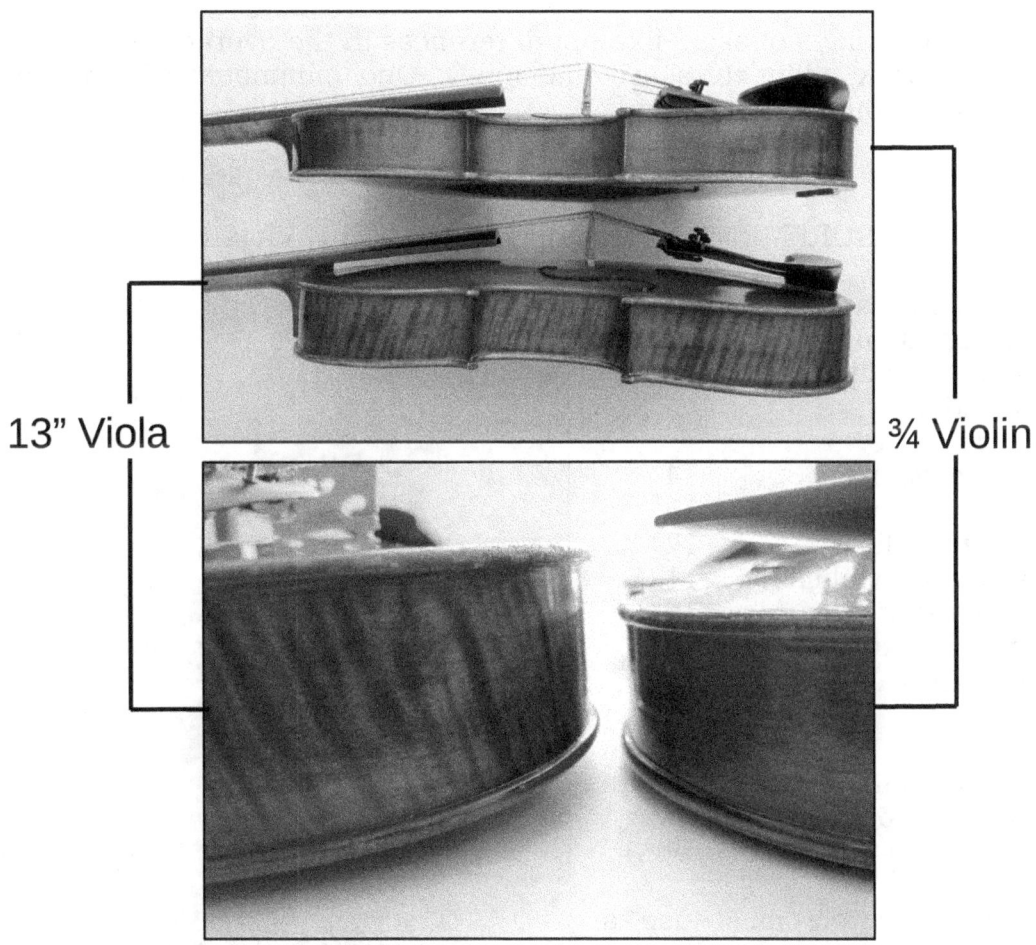

13" Viola   ¾ Violin

Luthiers measure in metric, but I don't know what teachers have available, so I'm going to give ballpark measurements in both inches and millimeters for rough rib heights and how they differ. I am measuring the height of the rib down by the endbutton, NOT including the edges of the plates. Just the ribs themselves.

Full-size violin:	1 1/4"	(31mm)
14-inch viola:	1 3/8"	(35mm)
Three-quarter violin:	1 1/8"	(28mm)
13-inch viola:	1 1/4"	(33mm)
Half-size violin:	1 1/16"	(26mm)
12-inch viola:	1 1/4"	(32mm)

I know these may not seem like big differences to the average person, but in violin work millimeters are like miles. One millimeter of difference matters to luthiers a great deal

ROUGH MEASUREMENTS FOR DIFFERENT SIZED VIOLINS

Instruments are measured by body length on the back from next to the button, down to the lower edge.

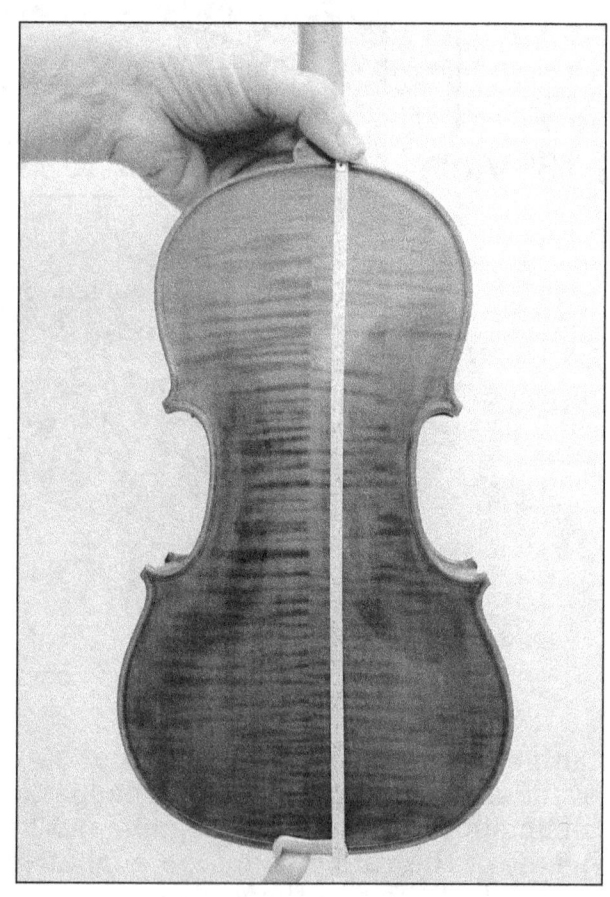

Full-size violins:	14"
Three-quarter violins:	13"
Half-size violins:	12"
Quarter-size violins:	11"
Eighth-size violins:	10"
Tenth-size violins:	9 ½"
Sixteenth-size violins:	9 ¼"

Violas are not described in fractions, but with body length in inches, so they are easy. (A 12-inch viola is 12 inches, etc.)

If you absolutely must use a violin as a viola smaller than 12 inches, I recommend leaving on violin strings (so as not to damage the string slots on the bridge or nut) and tuning the top three strings down and leaving the G a G. (No, it won't sound good, but physics is against you anyway.)

TELLING DIFFERENT KINDS OF BOWS APART

Violin bows have a distinct corner at the back of the frog.

Viola and cello bows typically have a rounded frog.

Cello bows are heavier, thicker, and shorter than viola and violins bows, and have a wider ribbon of hair.

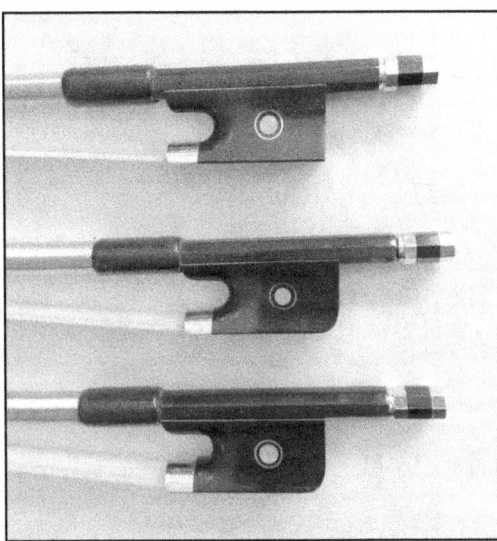

Violin

Viola

Cello

ROUGH LENGTHS OF BOWS FOR VIOLIN/VIOLA

I'm measuring these from the tip of the nose to the end of the screw. Bow lengths, particularly for the tiny violins, vary far more than people realize. These are rough numbers, and basically in a classroom as long as the bow fits the case and works for the student you will be okay.

But again, if you are simply sorting what you have and need to know what you are working with, this may help you organize a pile of bows:

Full-size violin/14-inch + viola bow:	29 3/8"	(74.8cm)
Three-quarter size violin/ 13-inch viola bow:	27"	(68.5cm)
Half-size violin/12-inch viola bow:	24 1/2"	(62.2cm)
Quarter-size violin bow:	22"	(56.0cm)
Eighth-size violin bow:	19 1/2"	(49.5cm)
Tenth-size violin bow:	18 1/2"	(47.0cm)
Sixteenth-size violin bow:	16 3/4"	(42.5cm)

ROUGH LENGTHS FOR DIFFERENT SIZED CELLOS

Again, measured by body length from the back.

Full-size cello: 29 3/4"   (75.8cm)
Three-quarter cello: 27 1/4"   (69.0cm)
Half-size cello: 25 3/4"   (65.4cm)
Quarter-size cello: 22 3/4"   (58.0cm)
Eighth-size cello: 20 3/8"   (51.8cm)

ROUGH LENGTHS FOR CELLO BOWS

Full-size cello bow: 28 1/4"   (71.7cm)
Three-quarter cello bow: 26"   (66.0cm)
Half-size cello bow: 24 1/2"   (62.0cm)
Quarter-size cello bow: 22 3/4"   (58.0cm)
Eighth-size cello bow: 19 3/8"   (50.0cm)

SIZING INSTRUMENTS ON LITTLE KIDS

There are a number of ways to do this, but here's what I think makes sense for the average school:

For violin, have several sizes out to try. When a child is standing up straight with an instrument tucked properly under the chin, they should be able to cup the scroll in their left hand while still having a decent amount of bend and slack in the arm. If their arm is out straight in order to reach the scroll, go down a size and look at that. If they look really cramped, go up.

Take finger length into consideration. Just because a student has long enough arms for a particular size, doesn't mean they have the finger reach, and you'll have to compromise until they grow.

In our rental program, the average first-grader usually needs an eighth-size violin, third-graders around a half-size. Nearly all kids by the time they are eleven or twelve are in a full-size.

Viola sizing is a little more fluid, but for beginners most people use the corresponding violin size. A kid who measures out at a half-size violin would use a 12-inch viola, etc. Beyond a 14-inch, it's whatever size they can handle comfortably. Don't push kids into too big a viola too soon. I check people on violas that are 15 inches or larger by having them place all their fingers on the instrument in first position, then see if they can do a reach-up (shift their 4th finger a half step higher than first position) without dislodging the rest of their fingers. If they can't easily do a reach-up, I recommend they stay in the smaller size. Most adults end up playing a 15 ½ or 16-inch viola.

For sizing a cello, the advice I hear usually centers around the player's left hand. Height adjustments can be made with the endpin, but the hand needs to be able to stretch comfortably. When placing their hand in first position on the neck, the player should be able to lay down all four fingers at each half step without undo effort. Check where the back of the cello meets the player's sternum, and the pegbox in relation to their head and see what looks reasonable and comfortable.

All the cello teachers I talked to agreed that it's better to play an instrument that is too small than too big.

A (VERY) FEW NOTES ABOUT BASSES

Basses are a whole different animal, and many of my tools and techniques do not transfer to them adequately. As I mentioned back on page one, someone else will have to write that book. However, I did consult people about basses, and if you are lucky enough to have some bass players in your orchestra room, here are a few things unique to those instruments that you should be aware of:

Basses have tuning machines instead of pegs. To keep those gears running properly, you need an oil applicator.

Many bass bridges have adjusters in the legs. These can cause added flexibility to the bridge, which means you need to check for bridge straightness more frequently since that added weakness means they are more inclined to lean.

When using the adjusters, it's important they both be raised and lowered equally. Trying to raise only one side will cause the bridge to tilt and create problems.

SHOULDER RESTS

Your violin and viola players must have them. Even if all you can offer is a basic sponge to provide enough friction to keep instruments from slipping, you can't start kids off playing these instruments without something to use as a shoulder rest. It's worth the expense and trouble, because otherwise you are spinning your wheels trying to get new players to hold their left arms in the proper position (they shouldn't be trying to support their instrument with that hand, which causes them to bend their wrist), or to bow properly.

Players must ALWAYS remove shoulder rests or sponges from their instruments before shutting them in their cases. I don't care how thin the sponge is. TAKE IT OFF. I've lost count of the number of instruments I've had to give a death sentence to because someone crushed the top of their instrument in the case when they left the shoulder rest on.

CASES

This one is tough since there are so many kinds of cases out there, but I can at least give you my take on cases in general.

The most common type I see in schools is those shaped hard cases with two or three latches. I don't like these. As a luthier, I see a lot of damage caused from their inadequate protection. Since they are hard on the outside, they are deceptive. Kids are more likely to treat them roughly than a case that looks comparatively fragile. But because the interior of the case has no suspension (meaning there are no supportive structures keeping the back of the instrument from sitting directly against the back of the case), knocking the case around can cause serious problems, including moving the post and bridge through inertia.

The bow latches inside these cases often fail as well, and if you don't have some kind of cloth in the case to protect the instrument when that happens, you can end up with some nasty scratches.

I don't have much advice about maintaining these kinds of cases because they are too cheap to do much with. My best tip would be to maybe have each kid who uses one bring in some sort of old t-shirt to use as a violin blanket and a cleaning cloth, and have an exercise where everyone writes basic rules on it to remember about using their instrument. (Loosen your bow when you put it away, rosin your bow before you play, remove your sponge before you put your instrument in the case, etc.) The extra bit of padding in the case could be the difference between needing a repair and avoiding one.

Given the option when purchasing cases, find something with SUSPENSION, and a ZIPPER. Latches fail, instruments fall out…. Zippers eventually go bad, too, but people don't bother to put instruments back in cases with bad zippers. People do take risks with bad latches.

Better cases are worth the expense over time because it saves you in repair costs later. And I've seen some good basic cases that are affordable and much better than shaped hard ones. It's worth doing some searches.

For better suspension cases, I keep a supply of parts salvaged from broken ones to do repairs with. Bow holders, zipper pulls, handles, latches, blankets, etc., can be unscrewed, ripped out, and put onto another case if you are handy with a drill and a hot glue gun.

BOW BUGS

If you have bows enclosed in storage in the dark for long periods of time, you need to take precautions against bow bugs. (See pages 37-38.)

HUMIDITY and TEMPERATURE CONTROL

The ideal relative humidity level for violins is between 40 and 60%. When violins get too far outside of this range they can be in danger of cracking or opening seams.

I prefer to monitor this within the general environment of the room where an instrument spends the most time, but older more fragile instruments, or instruments that travel rapidly and often from one kind of environment to another, may need more specific ways of adjusting humidity in closer proximity to the instrument itself. This usually means some kind of way of adding moisture to a case, and a hygrometer to give you a humidity level reading. Most instruments kept in consistent and comfortable environments don't need additional care in this area.

Personally, I'm not generally in favor of devices designed to increase humidity inside the body of the instrument itself, simply because I've seen too many accidents where a leak caused damage. If you have questions about individual instruments and their humidity control needs, talk to a local luthier about what they recommend in your particular climate for your specific instrument.

When storing instruments at school, in colder climates you must have a humidifier in the classroom and the store room during the winter. You can save potentially thousands of dollars of damage by simply making sure instruments are not subjected to extreme and harmful conditions in your school.

I knew one college that shut off heat to its cello room over winter break every year, and every time the instruments would come out of that looking like they had lost a bar fight. Insisting the school leave the temperature and humidity consistent in that room made a huge difference (and saved on repair costs).

It's important. Fight for it. Some schools will even find that money in the building maintenance budget and it won't impact what funds you have available to you in your program. Ask.

WORKING WITH A LUTHIER TO DO SCHOOL REPAIRS

Most school systems are not lucky enough to have an instrument specialist to work with. Most teachers are on their own in their individual school to manage a fleet of instruments by themselves as best they can.

I know when I keep repeating that bow hair needs to be replaced annually, that teachers in string programs in schools with no maintenance budget are rolling their eyes. I've seen the stockpiles of terrible bows with hair that is somehow expected to last decades, and that teachers are resorting to cleaning bow hair with alcohol when they get too filthy and simply rosining them up again to make due. Because the choice is that, or nothing. That's a horrible choice, and I'm sorry.

The biggest error I see organizations make that want to acquire violins for student use, is that they don't factor in a maintenance budget. They stop at the purchase of the instrument as if it was a one time expense. It isn't. It's more like buying someone a pet fish. You don't have to do a lot for it most of the time, but you can't neglect it. It still needs regular attention and there are continuing costs during the course of its life. Most people don't know this, particularly if they are not musicians themselves. Speak up. Explain your needs to the principal, to the school fundraising volunteers, and to the parents of the kids in your class. If people don't understand the problem, they can't help with a solution.

In the meantime, let's talk for a minute about how to work with a luthier to get the most out of the instruments and budget you've got:

In my experience, most teachers aren't sure what they actually have. In those cases, it helps to have someone come in and inspect the full inventory and make notes on everything. I charge a basic hourly rate to do that, and teachers find it worth the expense.

When I walk into a school for the first time, we lay out each instrument like we're in a trauma unit. I do quick assessments about which instruments need triage, which are relatively fine, and which are dead. Often teachers are surprised by which instruments I think are worth investing in. I've found violas from the 1930s that were literally falling apart and haven't been played in decades that were made of excellent materials and crafted well that deserved attention. I've seen brand new cellos that were simply built wrong enough that they could never be played and were not worth putting any money into at all.
Find out what you have. Then make a plan.

When I look at the instruments at a school, I give the teacher recommendations about what makes the most sense to do in what order, and set up a timeline and a list of priorities. Some years you need more violas, some years you don't. Maybe a bigger part of the budget goes into making sure there is one decently working cello because there is a particularly talented kid in that section at the moment. Assume your needs will change from year to year and plan to adjust.

Anything that is a simple fix, or is needed most, goes to the head of the line. Sometimes all a violin needs to work right is to have a bridge cut down, or a peg adjustment, or a simple seam gluing.

After that, there is usually a selection of things that need more work, such as gluing top cracks or fingerboards, in addition to a new bridge or a peg. Those we start on a schedule, where I'll do maybe half of those, and the other half the following year to spread out the cost.

Then there are the "piles of hope" where maybe the instruments are decent and should not be thrown away, but their needs exceed any normal school budget. I have fixed some of those for free simply because it was the right thing to do. But those are good candidates for charity. There are fund raising organizations and people for whom spending a few hundred dollars on making a violin play again is not hard for them to find money for, but they can't help with what they aren't aware of. And every once in a while a school will find a little extra cash in their budget and we add one of those instruments to the list of what gets fixed that year.

The last pile is the dead instruments. Anything where the instrument is too cheap to bother fixing because they have soundpost cracks or need a neck reset, can go. Cannibalize whatever parts you can. I keep a box of spare tailpieces and bridges and pegs I've salvaged from dead instruments from public schools, and I reuse whatever possible on other instruments in the system to keep their costs down.

Eventually, one by one, I get my hands on every violin in a school and bring them up to code. At that point we can focus on budgeting for a regular schedule of replacing strings and bow hair.

The key to working with a small budget is rotation. If you have 60 instruments in your program, I understand you likely can't afford new strings for them every year, even cheap strings. But maybe do 20 to 30 at a time, and schedule instruments to get new strings every two or three years. Just keep track of which instruments got what. It makes a huge difference compared to everything having decade-old strings.

Same with bow hair. Again, I know most schools can't get new hair on their bows every year, so aim for every two or three years, and schedule which instruments get what on rotation. It's also worth tracking down companies that do trade-ins on old bows. There are programs for exchanging used bows for new ones at relatively low cost. It's worth the effort, even if you can only do a few at a time.

In terms of finding a luthier to do cheap repairs, that can be a challenge. I know luthiers who cannot bring themselves to take short cuts or do things in a way that deviates from their training. I'm that way too, to an extent. I've turned customers away if the only repair they could afford was one I didn't want my name attached to. It's painful to have to do work the "wrong" way.

However, I am sincerely interested in making sure every kid who wants to play gets to play. Sometimes that means using epoxy in a way that makes me shudder. Often it means I put a set of used strings I have lying around the shop onto an instrument where new strings are not in the budget. It means a mantra of "good enough" and simply making sure the setup on a rotten instrument isn't interfering with a child's ability to learn.

Luthiers want instruments to work. We want people to play them. Talk to your local luthier if you are lucky enough to have one, and see what they can offer. Not all of them have the time or inclination to help in ways that are practical for your situation, but you don't know until you ask. And many may have ideas you haven't considered. For instance, even schools without maintenance budgets can write tax deduction letters for donations. I managed to repair nearly all of the violins and violas for a local high school over the course of a few years through tax deduction letters for my donated work. And now that the bulk of the instrument work is taken care of, they can finally use their budget for things like new bows and strings.

In the meantime, hang in there, and do whatever MacGuyvering you need to that keeps your string programs running. That's heroic work. And don't think just because I'm out here nagging about best practices, that I don't understand what you are dealing with. I get it. And I appreciate what you do for your students.

CHAPTER 9

ADDITIONAL DOs AND DON'Ts

DO:

Do allow time for an instrument to acclimate in the case when coming inside from extreme cold before opening it and exposing it to a much warmer environment. If your case comes with a bag to place your instrument into inside the case, the added protection can help with those temperature adjustments as well.

Do practice regularly for the health of your instrument. (Violins need to be played!)

Do ask for suggestions if something is uncomfortable about using your instrument. Learning to play can be awkward, but should never be painful.

Do remember to budget for basic maintenance as part of the cost of owning an instrument.

Do carry your instrument on a plane with you if you fly anywhere with it. (Checking it with baggage is a recipe for disaster.)

Do make sure to remove any kind of shoulder rest from the back of your violin or viola before closing it in the case.

Do always use the zippers on your case if it has them, as well as any "seat belts" inside that tie your instrument in place at the neck. (Latches fail. A shocking number of instruments are damaged by falling out of their cases, so don't neglect that simple step.)

Do make sure you have ways to identify your instrument if you get separated from it. An identification tag on (or inside) the case is a good idea, and take a couple of photos of your instrument to access if you need to show someone what your instrument looks like should it get lost or stolen.

Do remember to stop once in a while to appreciate how cool violins are in general. (They are really cool.)

Do seek out hands-on courses in repair if they are available to you and you want to know more. Even if you can't afford a good summer program, check out online tutorials from reputable shops.

Do come visit your luthier at least once a year. And bring chocolate. (Okay, you don't have to bring chocolate, but it's nice.)

DON'T:

Don't keep forcing a case to close if it feels like something is resisting.

Don't leave your instrument unattended in a car (due to extremes in temperature and risk of theft).

Don't shove anything into the f-holes. I know it seems like a convenient place to prop things that may help a student guide their bow, but it's not worth it. Even if as a teacher you've never had a problem with a straw or a stick or a pencil shoved into an f-hole eye or stem as a marker for someone to use as they play, parents and players often aren't so lucky when they try to repeat what you do. I see many f-hole cracks and damaged tops from this practice. Again, if you wouldn't do it to your own instrument (or a Strad) don't do it to someone else's.

Don't attach things to the instrument with hot glue. (You know I'm putting this here because I've seen it happen.)

Don't "wash" your instrument.

Don't try to disinfect your instrument with anything other than time. When we get instruments in the store that we have concerns may have been in a home with a person infected with a virus, we let it sit in quarantine for several days before handling it, and we wash our hands regularly when we finally do.

Don't write on the bridge. (It's only four letters students are trying to learn. Trust that they can do so without the bridge being defaced.)

Don't use an instrument as a hard surface to put paper on when you need to write something.

Don't store instruments in a basement or attic where there are issues with moisture, cold, heat or humidity.

Don't be afraid to ask questions. Luthiers have a reputation for being secretive, but thankfully that's changing. (In my shop, I'll happily talk your ear off about violins all day—assuming I'm not swamped with repairs at my bench and need to focus.)

Don't assume some repair is safe to try at home just because it looked good on the internet. I've seen some truly horrible demos on YouTube about doing things like replacing tailpieces yourself that made me really angry, because they are filmed well enough they look legitimate, but suggest things that can cause permanent damage to instruments—things even a luthier can't fix for you (at least, not affordably).

And finally:

Don't assume there is only one way to do things just because you read it in a book. Even this one. Repair techniques are always evolving, and there are things luthiers used to do as standard practice not long ago that no one would do today. And some methods vary wildly from shop to shop.

A great example of that would be straightening bridges.

I learned to straighten a bridge in a high-end violin shop. I was taught to soak it in body-temperature water for no more than 25 minutes, then steam it out by pressing it in a hot pan, flipping it repeatedly on the heat until it was dry, and finally letting it sit for another hour before putting it back on the instrument. If I got distracted and let the bridge soak too long, my boss was not happy. If I goofed and let the water get too hot, he was even more not happy.

Then a few years into running my own shop, a friend shared with me the method she was told to use someplace where she worked, where you didn't soak the bridge at all, but simply laid it on some folded wet paper-towel on a very hot metal plate where you pressed it to steam it out, then clamped it to a bench as it dried. This method works fine, and using it I can turn around a bridge straightening in about fifteen minutes if I need to.

But that's not the crazy thing. While preparing this book, I found out how other luthiers I know straighten bridges. One friend of mine soaks a bridge for 24 hours, then hangs it upside down to dry for an additional 24 hours. I also learned an accepted method in a different region of the country is to *boil* the bridge for several minutes. I've even talked to luthiers who involve a microwave in the process (which really makes me smile imagining what Stradivari would have made of that). And there are more variations, but these examples are sufficiently extreme to make my point.

My boss would have had my head if I'd let a bridge soak overnight, or boiled one. (I can't even picture what he would have done if I'd tried to stick one in the shop microwave.) But apparently it didn't matter. He had his way and he felt strongly about it. That's how shops work. Whatever luthier is in charge dictates the rules and you stick to them, so everyone is consistent and accountable. It feels as if there is only one way to do things in that circumstance, but it's not always true.

So, no, don't just take my word on everything. You will find luthiers who agree with all of what I've put in this book, and others who will object to certain parts. My experience, training, and thoughts are merely one part of a larger story. I will tell you if your bridge is warped, to take it to a luthier. But a different luthier may think you can fix it yourself. Investigate and decide which person's perspective makes the most sense to you in terms of your situation.

For the record, the main reason I am uncomfortable suggesting a player straighten their own bridge (despite the fact that apparently you can't go very far wrong while doing it), has to do with all the other things connected to removing a bridge from an instrument. Most people don't own a bridge jack or know how to safely use one. Many players don't have the resources to measure or mark the original bridge placement in order to return it back to its precise location. The post could shift or fall. It could be missed after straightening that a bridge may also need to be cut down. Most people don't have new parchment or drum skin to glue on. Etc., etc., etc. I see too many possibilities for how someone could get into trouble, and all I want is for your instrument to be safe and sound.

I have shared here what seems reasonable from my perspective, but I am cautious with other people's equipment. I've seen too many unfortunate things to be quick to let people without enough experience do much on their own. That doesn't mean you can't learn to do real repairs, just find a person you trust to show you a good way. Read more books. Take a course. Talk to people. Then use your own best judgment and your gut and your heart.

CHAPTER 10

RECAP OF BASIC MAINTENANCE

I considered putting a list of basic violin maintenance and the kind of schedule for it at the beginning of this book, but I think it makes more sense here at the end. Because if you've read everything up to this point, you will understand all of these terms, and I can talk to you the way I would to an informed colleague without having to stop and explain everything.

• Wipe your instrument down with a soft dry cloth after you play, rather than let rosin build up on the strings, fingerboard, and top.

• Always loosen your bow when it's not in use.

• Never loosen all your strings unless there is some emergency that requires you to remove the extra tension from the instrument (such as if the post has fallen or the neck has come loose).

• Never touch your bow hair.

• Try not to touch your varnish too much.

• Make sure your hands are clean before handling your equipment.

- Get your instrument an annual checkup. I suggest to my customers that they give their violin an arbitrary birthday so it's easier to remember. When I see an instrument on a regular schedule, I can spot any changes more quickly, and usually before potentially big problems can arise. (For instance, I'd much rather prevent a bridge from warping than have to make a new one, and that's harder for me to do if I only see an instrument once a decade.)

- As part of that annual checkup, replace your strings and get a rehair. Both things make playing easier and more enjoyable, so better to put them on a consistent schedule than put them off.

- Regularly check that your bridge is standing up straight, especially during the first week with new strings.

- During annual checkups, a luthier should inspect the seams, the pegs, the board and nut, the string heights, the straightness and placement of the bridge, the placement of the post, the endbutton, and any varnish wear particularly on the edges and shoulders, along with doing a basic cleaning if necessary. You shouldn't need these things adjusted very often, but it's good to be prepared to have at least one of these things addressed each year. Most luthiers will know to do all these things if you simply say, "Do whatever it needs," but if you're unsure, ask.

I hope this book has been helpful. I love violins. I love this work. Thank you for making music and giving me a reason to do what I do.

ACKNOWLEDGMENTS

This book has been in the back of my mind for many years. I'm happy to answer questions in my store, but often wished I could simply hand people that information to read on their own and share with others. Originally, that bundle of information I was picturing was just a pamphlet, but the more teachers and players I talked with, the more information got added, until it eventually ended up the book you have in your hands.

The people I would first like to thank for their input on various drafts are Tim Detzer, Anna Huthmaker, Christopher Jacoby, Gretchen Leanna, Pamela Simmons, Robyn Sullivan, and Sarah Zawadiwsky. Their differing perspectives as either teachers, luthiers, or parents helped guide the final direction of this book. Thank you to Corey Swan for information on basses.

My husband, Ian Weisser, is not only my partner in life and my violin shop, but the person who figured out how to format this book with images. I'm not sure what I would do without him.

Thank you to my brother Barrett Klein for the cover design and his keen eye for proofreading.

Thank you to all the fine instructors I've been fortunate to learn from over many years, but particularly Brian T. Derber who taught me to build instruments, and the late Steven C. Haas who taught me how to repair them. (I wish he could have seen this book.)

I love being a luthier, and I love to write. I have really enjoyed having the chance to combine the two things in this endeavor. Thanks for reading. If you enjoyed it and want to check out my other writing, please visit my author page at korinthiaklein.com.

REFERENCES

Violin making and repair schools:

Chicago School of Violin Making, 3636 Oakton St, Skokie IL 60076

Violin Making School of America, 304 E. 200 S. Salt Lake City, UT 84111

North Bennet Street School, 150 North St, Boston MA 02109

Minnesota State College Southeast (Red Wing), 308 Pioneer Rd, Red Wing, MN 55066

Building and repair workshops:

Violin Craftsman Institute, University of New Hampshire Continuing Education, 24 Rosemary Ln, Durham NH 03824-3528

Learning Trade Secrets, https://www.learningtradesecrets.com

Oberlin Summer Violin Workshops, contact Anna Hoffmann at ahoffman@oberlin.edu

Repair guides:

Huthmaker, R.T. 2003. Uncovering the Myths of String Instrument Repair, a.k.a. Do I use bubble gum or duct tape or take it to the repair shop? Panormo Press, Atlanta, GA.

Strobel, H.A. 1989. Useful Measurements for Violin Makers, A Reference for Shop Use (fifth edition). Self-published. Aumsville, OR.

Books on violin making:

Derber, B.T. 2017. The Manual of Violin Making. Self-published. Presque Isle, WI.

Johnson, C. and Courtnall, R. 1999. The Art of Violin Making. Robert Hale (1700) Unknown binding.

Books on history:

Faber, T. 2004. Stradivari's Genius: Five Violins, One Cello, and Three Centuries of Enduring Perfection. Random House, New York, NY.

Hill, W. Henry, Arthur, and Alfred E. 1963. Antonio Stradivari: His Life and Work, second edition, Dover Publications, Mineola, NY,

Organizations:

Violin Society of America, 14070 Proton Rd, Suite 100, Dallas TX 75244
972-233-9107
infor@vsaweb.org

Federation of Violin and Bow Makers
c/o Jesse Maschmeyer
512 Van Ness Ave #203, San Francisco CA 94102
info@afvbm.org

For more on bow bugs:

Stinner, B. 2003. Wood borers and bow bugs. Journal of the Violin Society of America. 18(3): 123-142.

Johnson String Instruments. 2019. "Nasty bow-hair-eating dermestids can be eliminated." https://www.johnsonstring.com/resources/bitten-by-the-bug.htm Accessed 30 November 2019.

For a more complete overview of fine tuners:

violinist.com, 2018. "Violin Fine Tuners (a comprehensive catalogue)."
https://www.violinist.com/discussion/thread.cfm?page=1510
Accessed 30 November 2019.

To contact the author at her shop:

Korinthia Klein
Korinthian Violins
2900 S Delaware Ave
Milwaukee WI 53207
414-744-1350
www.korinthianviolins.com
kory@korinthianviolins.com

INDEX

after-length: 17, 72
back plate: 11
basses: 105
bass bar: 20
blocks : 21
bouts: 12
bow
    maintenance: 79-87
    parts: 28-38
bow bugs: 37-38
bridge
    cello: 90-91
    parts: 16-17
    placement: 15, 97-99
    standing straight: 55-59
    straightening: 115-116
button
    bow button: 36-37, 80, 84
    endbutton: 28
    neck button: 11, 102
buzzing: 43, 55, 69-78, 91, 97
camber: 32, 87
cello: 89-93, 104-105
cleaning: 66, 80, 99-100
chinrest: 24-25, 74
collar
    bow: 34, 85
    peg: 8, 50
corners: 12, 77
cracks: 14-15, 20, 24, 50-51, 86
daleks : 77
ebony: 9, 24, 34, 71
endpin: 92
ferrule: 35, 86
f-holes: 15, 19, 58-59, 76, 98, 114
fine tuners: 23, 43, 54, 72-73, 97
fingerboard: 9-10, 55, 75, 91
    dressing: 10
frog: 29-30, 34, 79-81, 103
glue: 13-14, 63-64, 70-71, 74, 77
graphite: 42, 92
hair: 30-31, 35, 37-38, 79-80, 83-85
headplate: 29, 86
humidity control: 107-108

imprinting: 26-28, 65-66
linings: 21, 76
luthier: 1-2 (and 3-121)
maple: 7, 12-13, 55
mortise: 29-30, 35-36, 80-82
neck: 11, 66-67
nut: 9-10, 42, 54, 60, 71-72
peg dope: 50-52, 96
pegs
    parts/use: 8-9, 43-46, 52-53, 74-75
    slipping/sticking: 47-51
pegbox: 7-9, 44-46, 50-53
    bushing: 9
plates: 12
plug: 30, 83-84
purfling: 22, 77
rehair: 31, 81-84, 93, 120
ribs: 13-14, 21, 70, 101
Romberg: 91
rosin: 31, 40, 79, 82, 119
saddle: 24, 77
screw: 36, 80-81, 83-85
scroll: 7, 50-51, 104
seams: 13-14, 70-71, 93
shoulder: 13, 66
shoulder rest: 26-27, 74, 106, 113
slide: 36
soundpost: 18-20, 60
spread wedge: 35, 83, 86
stick: 28-29, 32, 80, 87
strings: 39-47, 54-55, 66, 75-76, 91, 100
tailgut: 23-24, 53-54, 73, 91
tailpiece: 22-23, 42-43, 72-73
    Wittner: 23, 43, 97
tip: 28-30, 79, 83, 86-87
thumb grip: 34, 64, 81, 86
top: 12
varnish: 27, 65-68, 76, 99-100, 119
viola: 1, 41-43, 55, 73, 78, 91, 101-103
warping
    bow: 32, 87
    bridge: 17-18, 55, 59, 99, 114-116
wolf notes: 78, 92
wrap: 32-33, 85

www.ingramcontent.com/pod-product-compliance
Lightning Source LLC
Chambersburg PA
CBHW081114080526
44587CB00021B/3594